T0115203

MARRIAGE & FAMILY ALTER-COUNSEL

DR. SABELO SAM GASELA MHLANGA

WESTBOW
PRESS®
A DIVISION OF THOMAS NELSON
& ZONDERVAN

WestBow Press books may be ordered through booksellers or by contacting:

WestBow Press
A Division of Thomas Nelson & Zondervan
1663 Liberty Drive
Bloomington, IN 47403
www.westbowpress.com
844-714-3454

ISBN: 978-1-6642-3013-2 (sc)
ISBN: 978-1-6642-3014-9 (e)

Print information available on the last page.

WestBow Press rev. date: 04/14/2021

CONTENTS

PREFACE

Marriage and Family is the fundamental and fabric glue to bind the nation together and propel it to the mountaintop with culture and values as its DNA. However, it calls the family members and the nation's citizens to pull together and to honor and venerate God who is the source and giver of life. "Blessed is the nation whose God is the Lord…" (Psalm 33:12, NIV). It is in the context that this book, Marriage & Family Alter, presents the Christian core values and for family worship. The parents have a duty to educate, train, discipline, and to guide their children to be honorable, respectful, responsible and accountable for their actions, behaviors and hygiene. The same principles apply to the parents to be good examples and to live godly lives as role models to their children. The Biblical standards of Christian living is portrayed in the Scriptures and the parents are obligated to set good examples to their children. The family does not start with having children but a couple, a man and a woman, who love each other and are committed and are determined to start a family with mutual respect for each other regardless of their backgrounds.

Strong family foundation and the impetus of its force and energy drive the church and the nation to emphatic moral and spiritual efficacy. If the family is united, loving, caring and supportive to its members, it has a ripple effect to the community, society and to the whole nation. My profound gratitude goes to my lovely wife Judith and I dedicate this book to her for her patience, hardworking, being organized, loving and caring for me and our five children, Qhawelenkosi Blessing, Sinqobile Shalom, Thandolwenkosi Prosper, Nkosilathi Emmanuel, and Joseph Nkosana for their moral and spiritual support. The loving family of my friend Sheriff Brett and Jana Hightower with their four lovely children, Meredith, Emma, Malachi and Aryah, a family that puts us in the world map and the reason we became missionaries in the North West, Greater Seattle, in Kent. Pastor Tim Harris and his wife and WBC community, we owe them everything. The Bread of Life International Fellowship (BOLIF) members such as Dr. Barbara Sibanda, Nomasonto forgiveness Nxumalo, Leroy and his wife Milile Nyathi, Angela Moyo, Sibonile Sibanda, Patience Malaba, Professor Don Makande, Phetheni Ndhlovu and her son Sibusiso, Gerald and his wife Anna and their lovely children and many others. Our dear friends Haggai and Mary Habila and their children Magdiel, Mitchell and Haziel and their friend, Bonnie Brown. My gratitude goes to our dear friends Roosevelt and Ashleigh Fenelus, Elder Brooks and his wife Dayna Brooks, Albert and Priscilla Ndlovu, Mai Mukungatu, Russsell and Judith Chinyani, Sukoluhle and Fanuel Malunga, Mary Dempsey, Elijah and Natalie Moyo, Hamah and Future, Mai Makonese, Marsha and Mai Priscilla Mutisi, Rev. and Mrs. Guzha, Tafadzwa, Cosmas and his family, Nakai Bofu and his family, Loverage Guzha and his family, Sadock and Rudo Mashindi, Douglas and Wadzanai Gonde, Kuda Mashindi, for having been a tremendous support and inspiration to me and my family.

To the NWBC Church Planting team for their unwavering support, Tim and Kim Howe, Gary and Joyce Irby, Natalie Hammond, Randi Boyett and their team. To the PSBA team, Dr. Ron Shepard and his wife Patty, Tim Shepard, have been a great inspiration. To my friend Pastor Brian and Tina Duffer, Dr. John and Mira Cody, and SBC have been incredible supporters of the ministry, and Jonah and his wife and the Awakening Church, and Pastor James Appleby and his wife Merilyn (late). To all these lovely people I have mentioned above and those I have not mentioned, I am so grateful to all of them.

INTRODUCTION

CHAPTER ONE
GOD'S IDEA OF MARRIAGE & FAMILY

The Beginning of Creation

Marriage and Family Alter is a quest to present and preserve the Biblical model of marriage and family as presented in the Bible by God Himself. Marriage and Family is a sacred sanctity given by God to humanity and He set a standard to be followed by His creation, "That is why a man leaves his father and mother and is united to his wife, and they become one flash," (Genesis 2:24, NIV). The main thrust of the Scripture is to emphasize the man's separation from his parents and to start a brand-new home. The two become one flesh and naked to each other, which depicts transparent to each other in every situation, circumstance and everything in their disposal. One thing we must bear in mind is that because of the fall, there is no perfect marriage or family. What is a family? How does God define a family in the Bible? The definition of family in the Bible is different from society's definition of a family. Carl Henry asserts that, "The word 'family' is used to indicate not only a man with his wife and children, but also an aggregate of kinfolk, a community, a tribe, a clan, nation or even the human race. It is the oldest institution known, anating both the state and the church."[1]

Humanity operates out of the mercy of God as His creation. When a

---

[1] Carl Henry, Baker's Dictionary of Christian Ethics, (USA: Canon Press, 1973), 238.

couple marries, it has to understand that they are two sinners united but they need grace and mercy under the auspices and mercy of God. None of them is perfect and there should be no finger pointing because both are fallen beings. The cracks in their relationship, marriage and family should bring them together as they recognize their weaknesses and their need of the Savior in their lives and marriage. The Godhead relationship displays important portraits of marriage between husband and wife. The unity, the congruence in decision making displays a powerful solidarity in functional duties. In marriage and family, the couples are made aware about their special position as created in the image of God and His likeness. They are reminded that they are all fallen beings that they need the redeemer daily in their lives.

The church is the bride of Christ and Christ is the bridegroom. The church represents Christ on earth and is the body of Christ with all its diversity. The church continues the ministry of Jesus Christ to preach, teach, and disciple all those who confess Christ as Lord and Savior. The church has the responsibility to embrace everyone who comes to the church seeking the mercy of God, salvation, healing, and love, and who wants to be part of the body of Christ, regardless of nationality, creed, color, ethnicity and conditions. The church has an obligation to embrace and treat every human being with dignity, love, and mutual respect because they are created in the image of God. This chapter discusses the church's responsibility to treat all human beings as image-bearers (*imago Dei*), regardless of being considered outcasts in society.

The disobedience of the fall resulted in the redemption promise by an image-bearer to image-bearers. Jesus came as a perfect image-bearer to perfect other image-bearers. The disciples share the love of God in the world to all image-bearers as demonstrated by Jesus Christ. The Scripture reveals the need for the disciples to love, embrace, and care for those who are considered to be outcasts in the society. The Great Commission (Matt 28:18-20, NIV) compelled the disciples to preach and make disciples of all nations. The commission includes modern disciples continuing the legacy of making disciples in the diaspora and passing on the faith. In that one charge, the unity of the church has been solidified so that the evangelization of the entire globe will be realized.

Creation

Created in the Image and Likeness of God (Gen 1:26, NIV)

God created all things by his command; however, when God made man, as the crown of his handiwork, there was a dialogue within the Godhead. For God to create man at the end of all creation was an honor and favor. Before man was created, God completely filled the earth with vegetation and animals, a provision for man's survival. God created man with wisdom, unlike any created animals before him. The verse brings in the divine revelation of the Trinity. When God was creating, He said, "Let there be . . ." (Gen. 1:3, NIV) but when man was made, God made a consultation: "Let us make mankind in our *image*, in our *likeness...*," (Gen. 1:26, NIV). In creating the universe, vegetation and animals, God used authority and command, but it was with affection that he created man. The three persons of the Trinity consulted and concurred to make man. Mathews asserts,

> The creation account shows an ascending order of significance with human life as the final, thus pinnacle, creative acts, this is the only one preceded by divine deliberation ("Let us make" in (Gen. 1:26, NIV). This expression replaces the impersonal words spoken in the previous creation acts, (e.g., "Let there be," "Let the earth,"

Mathews drives the point that human life alone is special in the sight of God because man was created in the image of God and has a special place in creation.

Man was made in God's image and after his likeness. These two words express the same thing about *imago Dei*. When verse (Gen. 1:26, NIV) is examined closer, the interpretation of plural pronouns "let us," "our image," and our "likeness" (Gen. 1:26, NIV), draw attention to the identity of the Creator. Mathews continues,

> Regarding the verb "make," we have already observed at 1:1 that the verbs "made" (*asa*) and "created" (*bara*) are in parallel both structurally and semantically in 2.4a, b. Here the parallel between v.26 ("Let us make") and

v.27 ("So God created") indicates that they are virtual synonyms.[2]

The dialogue within the Godhead displays divine honor in creating human life. Gordon J. Wenham explains, "It refers to the 'fullness of attributes and powers conceived as united within the Godhead."[3] One would concur with the suggestion that it is the plural of fullness.

Wenham presents five views about the "image" and "likeness" in (Gen. 1:26, NIV) that need to be analyzed biblically and theologically. The first view he presents sees "image" and "likeness" as distinctive:

> According to traditional Christian exegesis (from Irenaeus, *ca*, 180 A.D.), the image and the likeness are two distinct aspects of ma's nature. The image refers to the natural qualities in man (reason, personality, etc.) that make him resemble God, while the likeness refers to the supernatural graces e.g., ethical, that make the redeemed godlike.[4]

"The image of God" is found four times in the Old Testament, (Genesis 1:26, 27; 5:3, and 9:6 (Gen. NIV). In (Genesis 5:3, NIV), the text says Adam fathered a son "after his image." Victor Hamilton argues, "The Hebrew word for "image" is *selem,* which the LXX normally renders by *eikon* (icon). . . .. Here *image* would be something conveying the idea of emptiness, unreality, insubstantiality."[5] This view may not express the original meaning of the text although, theologically, it may sound correct. The second view, by Wenham, suggests, "The image refers to the mental and spiritual faculties that man shares with his creator. The image of God resides in man's reason, personality, free-will, self-consciousness, or intelligence."[6] Scholars continue to refine the meaning of the terms

---

[2] Ibid. 160.

[3] Gordon J. Wenham, *Genesis 1-15*, Word Biblical Commentary, vol. 1 (Waco, TX: Word, 1987), 28.

[4] Ibid., 29.

[5] Victor P. Hamilton, *The Book of Genesis: Chapters 1-17*, The New International on the Old Testament (Grand Rapids: William B. Eerdmans, 1990), 134.

[6] Wenham, *Genesis 1-15*, 30.

"image" and "likeness" and they continue to find specific clues in Genesis to understand how the image was interpreted.

The third view, described by Wenham, contends,

> The image consists of a physical resemblance, i.e., man looks like God. The physical image is the most frequency word, *selem*. Genesis 5:3 Adam is said to have fathered Seth "after his image," which most naturally refers to similar appearance of father and son.[7]

The fact that both Old and New Testaments stress that God is Spirit and He is invisible diminishes this view. However, the view should not be dismissed outright because Jesus said, "If you really know me, you will know my Father as well…" (John 14:7, NIV). Jesus answered Philip's question about showing them the Father. There remains debate about whether Jesus was referring to his physical appearance or his spirituality that resembled his Father.

Wenham states the fourth view as "The image makes man God's representative on earth. That man is made in the divine image and is thus God's representative on earth was a common oriental view of the king. Both Egyptian and Assyrian texts describe the king as the image of God."[8] Wenham highlights that man was given power and authority to rule and subdue the rest of creation; man was created a little lower than the angels, crowned with glory, and made to rule the handiwork of God. "So when the woman saw the tree was good for food, that it was pleasant to the eyes, and desirable to make one wise, she took the fruit and ate" (Gen 3:6, NKJV). Gerhard Von Rad contends,

> Man has stepped outside the state of dependence, he has refused obedience and willed to make himself independent. The guiding principle of his life is no longer obedience but

---

[7] Wenham, *Genesis 1-15*, 30.
[8] Ibid., 31.

his autonomous knowing and willingness, and thus he has really ceased to understand himself as a creature.[9]

The author of Genesis puts emphasis on the creation of man—that they were created "male and female" (Gen. 1:27, NIV), which is a contrast with other creation stories in which gender is not mentioned.

Wenham's fifth view asserts, "The image is a capacity to relate to God. Man's divine image means that God can enter into personal relationships with him, speak to him, and make covenants with him."[10] Wenham points out that this view is supported by Karl Barth and Westerman: "Barth holds that the phrase 'in our image' modifies the verb 'let us make,' not the noun 'man.' There is a special kind of creative activity involved in making man that puts man in a unique relationship with his creator and hence able to respond to him."[11] The fifth view suggests that God created man in order to relate with him in a personal way. Out of the five views, the last view seems favorable because humans are the only created beings that can relate, talk, and make covenants with God. Man is a special creature that God intended to communicate with directly. Even though Adam and Eve disobeyed and rebelled against God's command, God rescued them from their predicament.

The scripture reveals and indicates that the image and likeness of God still remain in man even after the fall. That is why man is not all evil. The trails of God can be found in man and redeemable in Christ. The image and likeness of God makes man the crowns of God's creation of life. We have to put everything in good perspectives about the beginning of man, his fall and his redemption before we bring in the off-springs as a result of union and consummation.

---

[9] John H. Sailhamer, *Genesis*, in vol. 1 of *The Expositor's Bible Commentary*, ed. Frank E. Gaebelein, Walter C. Kaiser and Richard Hess (Grand Rapids: Zondervan, 2008), 69.
[10] Wenham, *Genesis 1-15*, 31.
[11] Ibid.

Created to Make Others Who Have God's Image and Likeness (Gen 1:28, NKJV)

God blessed Adam and Eve and said, "Be fruitful and multiply' fill the earth and subdue it; have dominion over the fish of the sea, over the birds of the air, and over every living thing that moves on the earth." God gave the human family the privilege and responsibility of taking care of all creation. As sin entered the earth, it negatively affected the prosperity of the earth and all living things in it.

God gave Adam and Eve two assignments: procreation and dominion. To all animals, God gave power to reproduce themselves. In Mesopotamia and Canaan, creation motifs were linked to fertility rites, and Genesis 1:28, NKJV puts that concept to rest. Reproduction is a God-given blessing and gift, which is not dependent on rites devoted to gods or idols. The purpose of God giving man a mandate to multiply and fill the earth was so that man would rule over the animals. God gave Adam and Eve a divine purpose for marriage: the procreation of children. It is God's purpose, will, and desire to bless his people with children and fill the earth. The blessing of God to be "fruitful" and "fill" the earth is the source from which human race emanate. John Calvin writes,

But here Moses would simply declare that Adam with his wife was formed for the production of offspring, in order that men might replenish the earth. God could have himself indeed have covered the earth with a multitude of men; but it was his will that we should precede from one fountain, in order that our desire of mutual concord might be the greater, and that each might the more freely embrace the other as his own flesh.[12]

In the same vein, it is in God's power, within his will and purpose, to allow some to be fruitful and others be barren. This barrenness might be the result of a medical condition, biological complication, or simply the will of the Lord. God is sovereign and He does what He wants for special purposes. Russel Reno alludes,

> The power of 'begetting" serves as the engine of history
> in Genesis and in scripture as a whole. The generations

---

[12] John Calvin, *Commentary on Genesis, Commentaries on the First Book of Moses*, vol. 1 (Grand Rapids: Baker, 1996), 97.

are the streams of forward movement. Procreation gives
us a future. . . As the command "be fruitful and multiply"
emphasizes, we are physically equipped to live in the image
of God, because we possess the potential for new life.[13]

To have a child is to have a future because children perpetuate the
family tree and become the next generation. The future of the law is carried
on to obedient children, as illustrated in Deuteronomy 6:6-7, (NKJV). The
angels were not made "male" and "female," for they were not to procreate
and propagate their kind (Luke 20:34-36, NKJV), but man was mandated
to do so to continue the race. Reno explains, "The *imago Dei* is found in
our giving birth to and nurturing children whom we cannot finally control.
Children become independent agents who eventually supersede us."[14] Reno
further discusses that procreation is not only biological reproduction,
but procreation is spiritual potential. Spiritual births of the children are
through witnessing and evangelization of the entire globe. New life in
Christ is procreation in the truest sense.

Created to Rule as God's Representatives (Gen 1:28, NKJV)

Man was created as God's representative on earth. Man is the crown of
God's creation and he has a special mandate bestowed on him by God.
He is accountable for everything on earth in the sky, the land, the waters,
the animals, and to other human beings, to be his "brother's keeper."
God mandated man to rule and subdue over all the living creatures of
the sky, and of the land and of the water. Air and water pollution, land
deforestation, and the killing of creatures to use their flesh as food was not
mandated. It was after the flood that domination in the consumption of
animals was extended to man (Gen. 9:3, NKJV). Hamilton propounds,

of the two verbs, *rada,* "exercise dominion," and *kaba,*
"subdue," the later connotes more force. Thus, it refers
to subjecting someone to slavery (2 Chr. 28:10; Neh 5:5;

---

[13] Russell R. Reno, *Genesis,* Brazos Theological Commentary on the Bible (Grand
Rapids: Brazos, 2010), 56.
[14] Ibid., 57.

Jer 34:11, 16), to physical abuse. . . All these references suggest violence or display of force. For reasons already indicated, it appears unlikely that we need to transfer the nuance of force and dictatorship into the use of *kabas* in Gen 1:28.[15]

Humankind should treat animals with dignity and take care of the environment, including water, air, and the land.

All creation was to be subdued by man as God's representative and God gave the humankind power to rule: "This is a place in which God has set man to be the servant of his providence in the government of the creatures, and, as it were, the intelligence of the of this orb, to be the receiver of God's bounty, which other creatures live upon."[16] Fruitfulness is dependent on God the creator. The Hebrew tradition was that love for earth was sacred and human righteousness was connected with the welfare of the earth. "A righteous man cares for the needs of his animal" (Prov 12:10a; 27:23; Deut. 25:4, NIV).

Fall

The Disobedience of the Fall (Gen 3:1-7, NKJV)

There was a mutual relationship and harmony between God and man before sin entered the human race through Satan's deception. God commanded, "Of every tree the garden you may freely eat; but of the tree of the knowledge of good and evil you shall not eat, for in the day that you eat of it you shall surely die" (Gen 2:16-17, NKJV). God alone knows what is good for man. In order for man to enjoy the "good," man must trust and obey God in every word that he spoke/speaks. When man disobeys God, he decides for himself what is good and bad. The serpent, the perpetrator of deceit in the garden, is mentioned as more, "crafty" (*'arum*) than any of the creatures. Sailhamer writes,

The description of serpent as "crafty" is in keeping with the fact there are several features of this story that suggest that the author wanted to draw a relationship between the fall and man's quest for wisdom. Man's

---

[15] Hamilton, *The Book of Genesis*, 139.
[16] Ibid., 140.

disobedience is not so much depicted as an act of great wickedness of a great transgression as much as it is an act of folly. He had all the "good" he would need, but he wanted more-he wanted to be like God.[17]

The forbidden tree is the knowledge of "good" and "evil." In the passage are two main subjects—God versus Satan—and Eve chooses to obey Satan rather than God.

The serpent speaks two times and that is enough to offset trust and obedience between man and his Creator. "Then the serpent said to the woman, you will not surely die. For God knows that in the day you eat of it your eyes will be opened, and you will be like God, knowing good and evil" (Gen 3:4-5, NKJV). The serpent implied that God was keeping his divine knowledge to himself. The serpent questioned God's command to man and challenged his credibility as the Creator. Both Adam and Eve participated in disobeying God's command not to eat the fruit from the tree of the knowledge of good and evil. Torre asserts, "The serpent is the first creature in the biblical text to objectify God, talking about God rather than talking to God or with God. Keeping God from the discussion, it is able to tempt the woman with a forbidden fruit."[18] The serpent was tempting Eve to disobey what God had commanded them to eat and not to eat in the garden. The serpent instilled doubt in Eve's mind and heart. When she disobediently ate the fruit, alienation between man and God occurred. Eve shared the fruit with Adam and immediately they discovered they were naked. The desire for food, the lust of eyes, and the quest for wisdom apart from God, compelled Eve to disobey God. "So, when the woman saw the tree was good for food, that it was pleasant to the eyes, and desirable to make one wise, she took of the fruit and ate" (Gen 3:6, NKJV).

The serpent purposely exaggerated and distorted God's prohibition to man that God was jealous, self-protective, and that he was cruel and an oppressor. Eve's response to the serpent is also exaggerated and contains distorted statements. Adam was given the instructions and the command before Eve was created. He distorted and exaggerated what God had

---

[17] John H. Sailhamer, *Genesis*, in vol. 2 of *The Expositor's Bible Commentary*, ed. Frank E. Gaebelein (Grand Rapids: Zondervan, 1990), 50.

[18] Miguel De La Torre, *Genesis, Belief: A Theological Commentary on the Bible* (Louisville: Westminster John Knox, 2011), 68.

said. She could not have understood clearly what God had commanded Adam; however, there is no excuse for sin. She added, "You shall not eat it, nor shall touch it" (Gen. 3:3, NKJV). She also does not mention God's statement, "You shall surely die" (Gen 2:17b, NKJV). Instead, she says, "Or you will die, (Gen. 3:3, NIV)." The serpent capitalizes on her oversight. John Walton asserts,

> First, a technical study of the syntax shows that the serpent knows enough to deny the precise penalty as God worded it. God's statement in 2:17, "You shall be doomed to death" is identified as an absolute infinitive coupled with the finite verb of the same root. To negate this sort of syntactical construction, the negative particle is placed between the two verbs forms, in effect negating the finite verb. . ... Instead, the negative particle precedes both verb forms, thus negating the absolute infinity. This construction occurs only two other times in the Old Testament (Ps. 49:8; Amos 9:8). Since the absolute infinitive serves in these cases to indicate the inevitability of the action, the negation of the infinitive absolute is a negation of the inevitability.[19]

The serpent paints the picture of God's statements, but they are a misrepresentation and distortion of God's statement to Adam. Both Adam and Eve were responsible for their sin against God.

The apostle John warns of adding or subtracting to the Word of God:

> "For I testify to everyone who hears the words of the prophecy of this book: If anyone adds to these things, God will add to him the plagues that are written in this book; and if anyone takes away from the words of the book of this prophecy, God shall take away his part from the Book of Life." (Rev 22:18-19, NKJV).

---

[19] John H. Walton, *Genesis*, The NIV Application Commentary (Grand Rapids: Zondervan, 2001), 204-5.

The warning tells that no one should ever distort or exaggerate the Word of God, either adding or subtracting from it; Eve and Adam included.

After eating the fruit, their eyes were opened immediately and they were conscious that they were naked (Gen. 3:7, NKJV). Their nakedness gave them shame. The knowledge they thought they would acquire after eating the forbidden fruit was not the knowledge they realized. Instead, they realized nakedness. They were ashamed of each other and God.

Adam and Eve's quest for wisdom, to be like God, was the pride of sin. When Adam and Eve saw that they were naked, they covered themselves with fig leaves, which was a temporary remedy to their problem. In providential grace and love, God sought them out and found them. He clothed them with animal skin. Man desired to be like God. They sought wisdom, but found vanity and toil.

Adam was crowned as the head and had been given the responsibility to assign names to all the animals (Gen 2:20, NKJV) and his wife (Gen 2:23, NKJV). They had sinned by disobeying God and were immediately experiencing the consequences of that sin. They began to put themselves in charge and covered their shame and nakedness with withering leaves that do not last. Hamilton contends,

> The verb sewed (*tapar*) occurs only more three times in the OT (Job 16:15; Eccl 3:7; Ezek 13:18). In Job 16:15 and Ezek 13:18 it means "to wear" (sackcloth, arm bands, i.e., some kind of clothing that is next to skin). Why the man and woman chose fig leaves is not clear.[20]

Some scholars believe that fig trees were the largest trees in Palestine, which is why the couple chose its leaves to cover themselves. However, they could not cover their shame and sin of disobedience.

The Consequences of the Fall—The Image Is Marred: Pain, Suffering, Death (Gen 3:16-19, NKJV)

The consequences of the fall have gross effects on all humankind, the animals of the forest, birds of the air, the ocean creatures, and the whole

---

[20] Hamilton, *The Book of Genesis*, 191.

universe. Sin distorted what God initially intended man to be and the image is deformed and twisted from its original form. Life changes for the worse; there is pain, suffering, and death because of sin. God pronounces his judgment for disobedience to man.

In verse 16, God pronounces judgment on Adam and Eve and on the serpent: "To the woman said, 'I will greatly increase your pains in childbearing; with pain you give birth to children. Your desire will be for your husband, and he will rule over you. (Gen. 3:16, NIV)." The woman is given two judgments: one related to child bearing and the other being overruled by her husband. First, God would increase pain and toil: she would give birth in agony. God created man and woman to enjoy the sanctity of good relationship in marriage, which was to be a source of blessing, but now was distorted by sin. When God created the woman, he did not talk about the pain the woman was going to experience. After the fall, God pronounces that he would increase the pain; "increase" meaning to add on something that already exists. Walton expounds,

> The noun translated "pain" in the first line is a word used only two other times in the Old Testament (Gen 3:17; 5:29). Nouns from the same root refer to pain, agony, hardship, worry, nuisance, and anxiety. The verb root occurs in a wide range of stems with a semantic range that primarily expresses grief and worry.[21]

The verbal root includes physical pain, which embodies psychological anguish. The pain and suffering she will go through is the consequence of her actions in submitting to the temptation and deceit of Satan.

The woman will experience anxiety in the process of conception to birth. Pain and suffering of a woman start with the anxiety of her ability to conceive and bear a child. If she conceives, she is bombarded by the anxiety of whether or not she will bear a healthy baby. She has worries throughout her pregnancy, including physical discomfort and her survival and the baby's survival at delivery. These are all strenuous pains and sufferings bestowed on the woman for her disobedience.

---

[21] Walton, *Genesis*, 227.

Second, her "desire" will be for her husband and he will rule over her. According to Hamilton, in Genesis, "The Hebrew word for *urge* or '*desire*' occurs only here and in Genesis 4:7. In the Canticles references it has a decidedly romantic and positive nuance, describing a feeling of mutual attraction between two lovers."[22] According to Walton, "desire" extends outside Genesis and

> occurs only two other times in the Old Testament (Gen 4:7; Song 7:10). This means that the synchronic database is slim, but that does not mean that it can be ignored. Gen 4:7 occurs not only in the same general context but also features similar circumstances on the syntax and discourse level.[23]

The woman's desire is to be dependent to the husband for fulfillment in her maternal instinct. The woman's desire is to have children and to be a mother. Relations between human beings suffer. McKeown states, "While human beings still enjoy some of the benefits of blessing such as the ability to procreate, they must contend with the new situation where the world and its inhabitants are out in harmony with the Creator."[24] Their lives changes forever and the relationship between themselves and God are marred.

Gen. 3: 7-19, NIV say, "Then to Adam He said, 'Because you have heeded the voice of your wife, and have eaten from the tree of which I commanded, saying, 'you shall not eat it': "Cursed is the ground for your sake; in toil you shall eat of it all the days of your life." The man's punishment for disobedience was expulsion from the Garden into hard labor for his survival. Robert Sacks writes,

The world outside the Garden is still that dry, hard land which required rain and a man to toil. After man had been formed, he appeared to be too

---

[22] Hamilton, *The Book of Genesis*, 201.

[23] Walton, *Genesis*, 228.

[24] James McKeown, *Genesis,* Two Horizons Old Testament Commentary (Grand Rapids: William B. Eerdmans, 2008), 37.

noble to be placed in such a position. God tried to rectify the situation by planting the Garden, but Man was incapable of leading such a life.[25]

Man could not freely eat of the produce provided by the Creator because the good and fertile land was cursed. God had given Adam and Eve freedom to eat from any tree of the garden except one. Man was to work and toil for his food for survival and to provide for his family. "Cursed is the ground because of you; through painful toil you will eat of it all the days of your life."

God's judgment matches the sin in the fact that the man's sin was that he ate (3:6, 12, NKJV). Hamilton points out,

> In response to man's trespass of eating, God speaks no less than five times of eating in his word to man (vv. 17 [3 times], 18, 19). Thus, the penalty on the man parallels the penalty on the serpent. To both God says a word about their eating. Similarly, God's word to the man parallels his word to the woman, for in the experiences of both there will be *pain* (Heb. *Issabon*). For her the pain will be connected with childbearing, and for him the pain will be connected with food. *Issabon* and the verb *asab* obviously refer to physical pain, but they also embrace the concept of anguish.[26]

God did not pass judgment on man as an external punishment that required physical labor and planning for his survival, unlike the woman who received internal pain and suffering from within her body. The woman would have pain and suffer as a mother and a wife and the male as a breadwinner and family provider. The judgment of man and woman are not temporary, but permanent situations until they return to the ground from where they came.

Sin began in heaven with the pride of Lucifer, not on earth. Adam and Eve succumbed to temptation and the results were disastrous. Judgment from God came in three parts: a war between the woman and the serpent,

---

[25] Robert D. Sacks, *A Commentary on the Book of Genesis,* Ancient Near Eastern Texts and Studies, vol. 6 (Lewiston, NY: Edwin Mellen, 1990), 35.

[26] Hamilton, *The Book of Genesis*, 202.

the woe on the woman on childbearing and as mother and wife, and work for man to toil and labor for food in the field to provide for the family. John Philips states, "But the curse went beyond the serpent to Satan himself. God asked no questions of him. In that declaration of war Adam and Eve heard the gospel message for the very first time."[27]

"In the sweat of your face you shall eat bread till you return to the ground, for out of it you were taken; for dust you are, and to dust shall return" (Gen 3:19, NKJV). Death was judgment, which was devastating to Adam and Eve, for when they were created, they were to live forever. Adam was created from the dust, the earth, and because of the sin of disobedience, he would die and return to earth from which he came. Returning to the earth was a separation between God and man. John Gill explains,

> His body was composed of the dust . . . and should be reduced to that again by death, which is not an annihilation of man but a bringing him back to his original' which shows what a frail creature man is, what little reason he has to be proud of himself, when he reflects from whence, he came and whither he must go.[28]

Death was both physical and spiritual, and God's relationship with man was different because of Adam's disobedience. Physical death brought about pain, suffering, murder, war, hunger, disease, and hate as the result of sin through Adam and Eve. Spiritual separation from God means there is no longer direct communication with the Creator. There is no spiritual connection between God and man because sin separated them.

Adam and Eve became the parents of a race of sinners throughout the ages. Rice asserts, "The taint is in the blood. The curse is on every cell of their bodies. The curse will be on every child they shall bring forth

---

[27] John Phillips, *Exploring Genesis, John Phillips Commentary Series* (Chicago: Moody, 1980), 61.

[28] John Gill, *An Exposition of First Book of Moses Called Genesis* (Lebanon, MO: Particular Baptist, 2010), 67.

and every descendent down through the millenniums."[29] Rice reiterates that every fabric of the human body is sinful and deserves death. Sin not only corrupted and distorted the human body, but it altered his spiritual composition as well. Sin brought disastrous effects to human physical and spiritual composition. Adam and Eve died both physically and spiritually. "Therefore, just as through one-man sin entered the world, and death through sin, and thus death spread to all men, because all sinned" (Rom 5:12, NKJV).

The Consequences of the Fall—The Image Is Marred: Separation from God (Gen 3:22-24, NKJV)

Sin separated man from God and the relationship between God and man was broken. The sin of rebellion and disobedience made God angry, and the mutual relationship that previously existed between God and man was tainted. "Then the Lord God said, 'Behold, the man has become like one of Us, to know good and evil. And now, lest he put out his hand and take also of the tree of life, and eat, and live forever" (Gen. 3:22, NKJV). The Lord expelled him out of the Garden of Eden to till the ground from which he was taken. John Marks contends,

> Man has stepped outside the state of dependence, he has refused obedience and willed to make himself independent. The guiding principle of his life is no longer obedience but his autonomous knowing and willing, and thus he has really ceased to understand himself as creature.[30]

Man was destined to death after the sin of disobedience. However, even though man was driven out of the garden and prevented from approaching the tree of life, God still loves and shows mercy toward him.

Herbert Leupold draws attention, "Whereas in (Gen. 3:8-21, NKJV) we had the substance of what God spoke to man in mercy and in judgment,

---

[29] John R. Rice, *Genesis: "In the Beginning . . ."* (Murfreesboro, TN: Sword of the Lord, 1975), 143.

[30] Gerhard Von Rad, *Genesis: A Commentary*, trans. John H. Marks (Philadelphia: Westminster, 1961), 94.

we have in (Gen. 3:22, NKJV), the persons of the Holy Trinity in divine counsel among themselves."[31] Leupold writes,

> But since, to the best of our knowledge, no tree of itself can possess such virtues, it seems best again with Luther to assume that this remarkable power was characteristic of the tree not by its inherent natural qualities but by virtue of the power of the Word of God, who was pleased to ordain that such should be the effect of partaking of the fruit of this tree. For man in his fallen and sadly altered state the acquisition of the quality of imperishability for this sin-torn and sin-defaced body would have a grievous calamity.[32]

It is imperative to understand that had man eaten of the tree of life, Christ's work to restore fallen man would not have been feasible, bearing in mind that man would be like God and live forever. Although death was the ultimate result of the fall, God in His sovereignty prepared the redemption of fallen man through Christ Jesus.

God had compassion and mercy for man. He wanted to save His creatures from the power of sin. Phillips writes,

> God moved in to rescue the wretched creatures who had fallen so low. He did so first in *grace* (3:20-21), for salvation is always through grace. Adam had discovered that the fig leaves of his own self-effort would not do in the presence of God. . .. There, in Eden, in paradise itself, blood was shed for the very first time. . .. It was the first dramatic illustration of the ultimate cost of Calvary, of the horror and dreadfulness of sin. Sin is a radical disease, and it calls for a radical cure.[33]

---

[31] Herbert C. Leupold, *Exposition of Genesis Chapters 1-19,* Christian Classics Ethereal (Grand Rapids: Baker, 1950), 180.

[32] Ibid., 181.

[33] Phillips, *Exploring Genesis,* 63.

Adam and Eve could have seen the gruesome death of the slaughtered animal for their covering instead of their fig leaves covering, signifying the first test of the gruesome death of Christ for the shedding of blood for sinners. Phillips reiterates, "To rescue the fallen pair God acted not only in grace, but He acted also in government"[34]

It was in God's mercy and grace that he drove them out of the Garden of Eden and prevented them from eating of the tree of life. God showed unbelievable love to fallen man. God made sure that Adam and Eve would not eat of the tree of life by placing guards, the Cherubim, at the east of the Garden of Eden, and a flaming sword that turned every way, to guard the way to the tree of life. Phillips explains,

> If Adam and Eve, in their fallen condition, had eaten of that tree, they would have lived forever in their sins. They would have become like the fallen angels, incapable of death and forever locked into the guilt and penalty of their sins. It would have been impossible to renew to repentance. God in His government did not allow that to happen.[35]

One would agree with Phillips in his analogy about the fallen angels who are not capable of repenting and being redeemed. God did not want human beings to have the state of fallen angels.

In God's command, the Cherubim, in contrast to the fallen angels, were God's representatives. The Cherubim are God's angels whom God uses in His government to accomplish His purpose in the world (Ps 18:10, NKJV). Leupold writes,

> The root from which the word may be derived would suggest that the word as such means "a brilliant appearance" (*glanzerscheinung*). How these marvelous beings appeared was well remembered by the Israelites at least, for they seemed to require no further description

---

[34] Ibid.

[35] Phillips, *Exploring Genesis*, 64.

when they were told to make two cherubim upon the mercy seat of the ark of the covenant and otherwise to use the figures of the cherubim for ornament purposes, (Ex 25:18; 26:1).[36]

The separation of God and man because of the sin of disobedience was disastrous, yet God did not give up on His creatures. The fundamental question to be posed is, are there some traits of *imago Dei* in God's fallen creatures? The next section explores and discusses whether or not the image of God is still in man.

The Image and Likeness Remains (Gen 5:1-3, NKJV)

Scriptures reveal that the image and likeness of God remained in man even after the fall. As a royal representative of God, man is still the only crown of life of God's creation. Genealogy is the perpetuation of the original:

This is the book of genealogy of Adam. In the day that God created man, He made him in the likeness of God. He created them male and female, and blessed them and called them Mankind in the day they were created. And Adam lived one hundred and thirty years, and begot a son in his likeness, after his image, and named him Seth, (Gen 5:1-3).[37]

Being the original created being in the image and likeness of God and representing God, God commanded Adam to procreate with Eve for his off springs resembling him. Hamilton propounds,

Vv. 1b-2 are introductory superscription that describes the cause of the effects detailed in the following verses. That Adam reproduces himself through Seth, and Seth through Enoch, etc., demonstrates that God's blessing has become effective. They are not only created in by

---

[36] Leupold, *Exposition of Genesis*, 184.
[37] Leupold, *Exposition of Genesis*, 184.

God but blessed by God. Such blessing is manifested in multiplication. It is appropriate that the creation of man be prefaced to Adam's descendants through Seth rather than through Cain.[38]

The contrast of God creating Adam, and then Adam reproducing himself in his son, Seth, is an illustration of a divine and natural phenomenon. It is interesting to see God perpetuate His image and likeness in man. Hamilton continues, "Furthermore, the reference to Gen. 1 at the start of this chapter permits a contrast between a divine creative act and human creative acts. In a sense Adam and his posterity are doing what God did. He created and they are procreating."[39] After creating them male and female, God blessed them and charged them to multiply and fill the earth. The divine image and likeness are transmitted from generation to generation with the genealogy of the firstborn son. In tracing the account of human sin and death, one can also see the continuing effects of sin and God's promise of procreation and blessing from the beginning. God preserves Adam's seeds through procreation as He promised and blessed him.

Based on God's promise and blessing to be "fruitful and fill the earth" (Gen 1:26-28, NKJV), Adam and Eve fulfill that promise. Mathews explains,

> It shows the evolution and universality of human wickedness, which deserves God's angry reprisal (6:1-8), but again, despite this, the hope that rests in God's favor toward Noah (5:29; 6:8-9) . . .. Although these two lines of descents have superficial similarities, they also present a stark dissimilarity. There is no linkage between Cain and Adam in the formal genealogy (4:17-24). The connection is derived only from the earlier narrative at 4:1. In the Sethite listing the setting of creation is preeminent (5:1b-3) for the purpose of cohesion between Noah and first

---

[38] Hamilton, *The Book of Genesis*, 255.
[39] Ibid.

things (Adam). Cain's connections with creation, on the other hand have been discounted-he is disowned! -and the rite of passage for blessing will be through Abel's successor, Seth.[40]

The omission of Cain in the genealogy is to look for hope and blessing in the future through the family line of Seth instead of Cain. Cain was the first born, but he did not inherit any right to the promise because of his actions—Seth is awarded that right. The image of God still exists in man; however, it is no longer a perfect image, but an imperfect image and likeness. McKeown asserts,

> If 5:1-3 is read without considering its context, the reader will almost certainly conclude that human beings are no longer in the image of God. Thus, whereas the Creator makes Adam in his own image-the image of God—Adam had a son in *his* own image. As God created man, in his own perfect image, so now, sinful Adam has a son in his own imperfect image.[41]

Adam passes his own image to his younger son, Seth, for Cain was rejected in favor of Seth. The image in man makes him superior to all the animals, even after the flood (Gen 9:6, NKJV). This proves that the image of God was not withdrawn, even if man sinned and fell short of the glory of God.

The image and likeness of God in man makes man still the crown of life of all the creation on earth. In his imperfect and sinful state, man still has dominion and rules God's creation. McKeown explains, "Now, in contrast, the effect of God's image in people and of his continued blessing on the human race is in focus through the progeny of Seth."[42] According to verse 3, Seth has his father's image and likeness. There is no biblical support to say that God withdrew His image and likeness from man when he disobeyed. However, there is evidence of imperfection in man because of

---

[40] Mathews, *Genesis 1-11:26*, 296.
[41] McKeown, *Genesis*, 45.
[42] Ibid., 46.

sin (Rom 3:23, NKJV). Cain's family genealogy purports humans moving away from God while Seth's family genealogy aligns toward restoration and building the broken relationship with God. Reno writes,

> Seth is enrolled with Adam in the project of physical survival that brings death as its future. . . Thus, the genealogy flowing from Adam gives us a picture of a fresh but failed effort to escape the gravitational force of the first sin. Even as the genealogy begins anew with Seth, he and his descendants slowly but inevitably trace a declining arc toward the target of death.[43]

The image and likeness of God in Adam is passed on to Seth from generation to generation. Adam's descendants embody sinful imperfections, and the result is death.

However, God planned for redemption and restoration through God-man, Jesus Christ, the Savior of the world. God's grace and love for created beings was so powerful that He gave His only Son to die on the cross for sins. The next section discusses the redemption of sinful man to salvation through Christ Jesus.

Redemption

Redemption Promised by an Image-Bearer for Image-Bearers (Gen 3:15, NKJV)

"And I will put enmity between you and the woman; and between your seed and her seed; he shall strike your head, and you shall bruise his heel" (Gen 3:15, NKJV). The judgment of God to the woman and her seed versus the serpent and its seed is very dramatic. The two parties involved would be enemies. The seed of the woman would bruise the head of the serpent and the seed of the serpent would bruise his heel. This was prophetic for the virgin birth. In general, the ancient world believed that only man could deposit the seed and a woman would be only an incubator

---

[43] Reno, *Genesis*, 112.

until she gave birth. The prophetic message was the virgin birth of Jesus Christ (Luke 1:1-36, NKJV). Walton expounds on the seed:

> The word "seed" is a collective noun that typically takes singular pronouns standing in its place. Therefore, when the text says *he* will crush your head, grammar cannot determine whether this is a reference to the corporate seed or one representative from among the descendants. The use of the singular "you" ("your head" and "you will strike") has sometimes been considered an indication that this must refer to Satan because the serpent does not continue to exist through the generations.[44]

The conflict is between the seeds of the two parties involved. The war between them is formidable and required one of them to win. In the history of the church, it has been believed that the seed of the woman is Christ and has defeated Satan at Calvary. Walton suggests,

> The verbs "crush" and "strike" are now properly identified as belonging to the same root, *swp*. We must therefore conclude that the actions performed are comparable. For this reason, the translation of the verb should be fairly generic so as to be suitable to both a strike to the head and a strike to the heel.[45]

The strike on the head causes more damage than a strike on the heel. The strike on the head destroys the head and kills the seed of the serpent. The strike on the heel does not cause lethal damage. Leupold observes,

> This is too obvious to require lengthy defense; for when man steps on a serpent's head, a crushing result; but when the serpent strikes while the contest is on, only a sting on the heel or a bruising result. But at the same time a

---

[44] Walton, *Genesis*, 226.
[45] Ibid.

crushed head spells utter defeat. A bruised heel may be nursed till healed.[46]

The seed of the woman (Christ) crushed Satan entirely and destroyed him (1 Cor 15:55-57, NKJV). Continual bitter conflict between humans and the evil in the world and hostility between the serpent and the man still exist. Whenever man and serpent meet, there is always conflict that involves life and death. There is always struggle between man and serpent. The exegesis of the text finds a messianic prophecy—a reference to a final victory of the seed of the woman (*protoevangelium*).

Satan possessed the serpent as a tool for sin. The serpent became the symbol of sin for all mankind. However, the victory is guaranteed to the seed of the woman and the defeat of the serpent. One born of a woman would win the victory. Isaiah 53 designates the coming Messiah. Leupold writes,

> It should be clearly observed that his gracious promise is the opening of the sentence or doom that God pronounces. Even on the first pages of the Bible we are shown the face of God 'merciful and gracious, slow to anger and abundant in goodness and truth' (Exod 34:6). He delights in showing mercy. . . Grace, provocative of faith, precedes the sentence.[47]

The early church and the modern church believe the Messianic prophecy portrayed in (Gen 3:15, NKJV). The text depicts the coming Messiah born of a virgin, Mary. Leupold puts beautifully how Christ completed the task of crushing the head of the Satin:

> A significant New Testament, yet however, looms up very prominently and serves as the same purpose; after Christ's public ministry is officially inaugurated by the His baptism, He encounters the devil in a temptation, even as the first parents encountered him. This, first of

---

[46] Leupold, *Exposition of Genesis*, 166.
[47] Leupold, *Exposition of Genesis*, 168.

all, confirms the fact that the first tempter was the devil, but it more distinctly displays the first crushing defeat that the seed of the woman administered to His opponent. On the cross this victory was sealed and brought to its perfect conclusion. The cry, "It is finished," marked the successful completion of the task.[48]

The seed of the woman finally put an end to both the power of sin and Satan. All Christians are under the protection and guidance of Christ who conquered Satan and death that was brought by the sin of rebellion. The image-bearer brought salvation to image-bearers through His sacrifice and death on the cross. The Second Adam brought life unlike the first Adam who brought death. The next section discusses the redemption through Christ Jesus who came as the perfect image-bearer.

Jesus came as the perfect image-bearer (2 Cor 4:4; Col 1:15; Heb 1:1-4, NKJV). "Whose minds the god of this age has blinded, who do not believe, lest the light of the gospel of the glory of Christ, who is the image of God" (2 Cor 4:4, NKJV). Satan will continue to perpetuate evil influence until Christ returns to establish God's kingdom in the full (Gal 1:4, NKJV). Those who deny and do not believe in the power of the gospel cannot appreciate or fully understand the claims of the gospel, unless God through the Holy Spirit and the gospel enlightens them (John 3:3 NKJV). He is the prince of darkness and the ruler of the darkness of this world. He blinds, deceives, enslaves, and darkens hearts of the multitude of people in the world. He sways many to disbelieve in the gospel of Christ. Colin Kruse asserts,

> *The god of this age* refers to Satan, who is permitted to exercise a limited rule in the present age (John 12:31), a rule that will be terminated although with the coming of the new age at Christ's return. In the meantime, he is active in blinding the minds of unbelievers to the truth of the gospel.[49]

---

[48] Ibid., 170.

[49] Colin G. Kruse, *2 Corinthians*, Tyndale New Testament Commentaries, vol. 8, rev. ed. (Downers Grove, IL: IVP, 2015), 140.

Paul spoke about the veil over the Jewish contemporaries who could not understand their own Scriptures as well as other unbelievers. Satan also veils believers to deceive and misguides them in order to hinder God's work. Paul mentions that Christians may hear the gospel but not appreciate its truth because Satan blinds them. Kruse explains,

> Paul says that the gospel is the glory of Christ, *who is the image of God*. There may be an allusion here to the creation of human kind in Genesis 1:26 ('Then God said, "Let us make mankind in our image, in our likeness'), especially in the light of the fact that Paul does speak of Christ as the 'last Adam,' comparing (and contrasting) him with the 'first Adam' (I Cor 15:45-49; Rom 5:12-19) . . .. For Paul, Christ the is the image of God after the fashion of Adam as far as is his humanity is concerned and after the fashion of Wisdom as far as his transcendence is concerned.[50]

Christ is the image of the invisible God because He is co-essential with the Father. Christ is the image of God who reveals the Father. Christ demonstrates the power and wisdom of God and his grace and mercy for the salvation of all sinners. The gospel reveals the glory of Christ who is the image of God. The glory of Christ is His divine and human excellence centered in His personality. Charles Hodge writes,

> Christ, in his divine nature or as *Logos*, is declared to be "the radiance" of the Father's "glory" (Heb 1:3), to be in the form of God and equal with God (Philippians 2:6, and perhaps also Colossians 1:15). But here is the incarnate *Logos*, the exalted Son of God clothed in our nature, who is declared to be the image of God, because "all the fullness of the Deity lives" in him "in bodily form" (Colossians2.9).[51]

---

[50] Ibid., 142.

[51] Charles Hodge, *2 Corinthians*, The Crossway Classic Commentaries (Wheaton, IL: Crossway, 2015), 74.

Christ is the image of God incarnate and the perverted image in Adam is replaced by Christ's image, the perfect image. Christ is the full representation of God and the expression of the nature of God, making God visible in Him.

Colossians 1:15, NKJV, says, "He is the image of the invisible God, the firstborn over all creation." Christ is the divine nature in His works of creation and providence. He is in Himself the image of God; the true representation of God. Daniel Wilson contends,

> The word image is used in two senses in Scripture, as it is still in our ordinary language. It sometimes means any resemblance, slight or not, of another person or thing, according to the nature of the subject spoken of. So, Adam was created "in the image of God," not as fully resembling God, but bearing some faint likeness to him in 'righteousness and true holiness.'[52]

Christ is consubstantial with the Father and has the same nature, qualities, perfections, power, and essence as the Father. Wilson explains that Christ possesses the glory of God: "It teaches us that Christ the uncreated Word and Wisdom of the Father, is his perfect image and resemblance, his exact counterpart; possessing all his glory, attributes, perfection, and powers, as the natural and only-begotten Son of God."[53] Christ is the image of the invisible God. The image of God in Christ denotes His perfect quality with the respect of His substance, power, and eternality.

The Son is the Father's image in all things. Moule reiterates Christ's image of God: "Not that the reference of the 'Image' here is directly or primarily to our Lord's Body of the Incarnation, but to His being, in all ages and spheres of created existence, the Manifester of the Father to created intelligences."[54] Christ is the first born of all creation as the image

---

[52] Daniel Wilson, *Expository on Colossians, Verse-by-Verse Bible Commentary* (New York: Bible House, 1859), 73.

[53] Ibid., 74.

[54] Handley Carr Moule, *Studies in Colossians and Philemon* (Grand Rapids: Kregel, 1977), 77.

of God. He is the reflection of the Father and radiates the attributes of the Trinity. The deflected image of God in man that was marred in the fall is restored in Christ. He is the new Adam in perfect image, reflecting the glory of God in his divine nature.

In Hebrews 1:1-4, NKJV, is written,

> God, who at various times and in various ways spoke in time past to the fathers by the prophets, has in these last days spoken to us by His Son, whom He has appointed heir of all things, through whom also He made the worlds; who being the brightness of His glory and express image of His person, and upholding all things by the power.

John Phillips points out,

> In the person of the Lord Jesus, God found a perfect vehicle of expression. He simply translated Deity into humanity, or, as John puts it, "The Word was made flesh" (John 1:14) . . . Moreover, Christ is "the express image" of God. The phrase "express image" refers to something "engraved" or "impressed" as, for instance, a coin or seal that bears line for line all the features of the instrument making it.[55]

The incarnation was an expression of God to reach out to a fallen human kind in order to save it. The expression of God's image is engraved in Jesus.

The author of Hebrews elucidates how God's expression of His image was revealed in Christ. Phillips expounds on the expression of God's image in Christ: "The lines of Deity have been reproduced in Jesus' humanity; so, to find out God is like we need only look at Jesus. We can take the lines of Christ's personality and draw those lines on out into infinity and obtain a perfect concept of God."[56] Christ is God manifest and God in

---

[55] John Phillips, *Exploring Hebrews, The John Phillips Commentary Series* (Grand Rapids: Kregel, 1977), 21.
[56] Ibid., 22.

substance. He is the reproduction of God; He is the image of the invisible God. John McCarthy writes, "The word 'image' here is *eikon*, from which we get *icon*. *Eikon* means a precise copy, an exact reproduction, as in a fine sculpture or portrait. 'For in Him all the fullness of Deity dwells in bodily form' (Col 2:9)."[57] God has made known the glory of His character through Christ His Son.

James Haldane expounds, "By contemplating in Him the glory of the Lord, we are changed into the same image from glory to glory as by the Spirit of the Lord. This is the new creation in Christ Jesus, which is essential to our being His disciples."[58] The image and likeness, which was marred in mankind, was restored and inaugurated in Christ and then it was sealed. Those who believe in Christ are made whole through the work of the Holy Spirit. The shedding of the blood of Christ for the remission of sin was completed in Christ and expiated the anger of God. Christ reconciled mankind to God and He paid the price in full. The new creation infused to all believers is completed and sealed by the Holy Spirit.

Jesus came to perfect other image-bearers (Rom 8:29; 1 Cor 15:49; 2 Cor 3:18; Col 3:10, NKJV). "For whom He foreknew, He also predestined to be conformed to the image of His Son, that He might be the firstborn among many brethren" (Rom 8:29, NKJV). The word predestined (*prohorizo*) occurs six times in the NT (Acts 4:28; Rom 8:29, 30; 1 Cor 2:7; Eph 1:5, NKJV). Theologically, the essence of predestination indicates that God has the plan and the design, and has prepared salvation for those called by His name—they are called by God's purpose (*prothesis*). To be predestined is to be conformed to the likeness of His Son. MacArthur asserts,

> Foreknew. Not a reference simply to God's omniscience-
> that in eternity past He knows who would come to Christ.
> Rather, it speaks of a predetermined choice to set His
> love on us and established an intimate relationship-or

---

[57] John MacArthur, *Romans1-8, The MacArthur New Testament Commentary Series* (Chicago: Moody, 1983), 16.

[58] James A. Haldane, *Hebrews*, Newport Commentary Series, 2nd ed. (Springfield, MO: Particular Baptist Press, 2002), 13.

election. A Greek grammar, called the Granville Sharp rule, equates "predestination" and "foreknowledge."[59]

Predestination is God's foreknowledge of those who are God's own who will be conformed to be like Christ. The security of salvation of the believers is embedded in Christ and they have already been destined to eternity in Christ. MacArthur highlights,

> Predestined, literally, "to mark out, appoint, or determine beforehand." Those whom God chooses, He destines for His chosen end-that is, likeness to His Son. Ephesians 1:4, 5, 11, conformed to the image of His Son. The goal of God's predestined purpose for His own is that they would be made like Jesus Christ. This is a "prize of the upward call" (Phil. 3:14; Eph.4:13; Phil. 3:20, 21; Col. 1:28).[60]

Paul writes using the past tense as if it has already happened because for him it is already done with absolutely certainty. Price gives an interesting argument, "Christians who have borne-and continue to bear the image of the man of dust shall also bear the image of the man of heaven. This hope has its present counterpart in Paul's conviction that men in Christ already bear this image, though not visible."[61]

Conformity to Christ's image is not from human endeavor but through the sanctification of the Holy Spirit when believers are transformed into His image and likeness. The Holy Spirit perfects the saints into the image of Christ daily and prepares them for the day of the second coming of Christ in glory.

First Corinthians 15:49, NKJV, says, "And as we have borne the image of the man of dust, we shall also bear the image heavenly Man." In light of this text, Henry Ironside elaborates on the heavenly man:

---

[59] John MacArthur, *The MacArthur Bible Commentary* (Nashville: Thomas Nelson, 2005), 1533.

[60] MacArthur, *The MacArthur Bible Commentary*, 1533.

[61] James L. Price and Charles M. Laymon, eds., *Interpreter's One-Volume Commentary on the Bible* (Nashville: Abingdon, 1980), 811.

> There are also celestial bodies, that is, heavenly bodies, and bodies terrestrial, earthly bodies. Our Lord came into this world and took a terrestrial body, but after having made satisfaction for our sins on the cross, He came forth in resurrection in a celestial body, and in that body, He ascended through the heavens into the very presence of God. . .. His celestial body is the pattern of what ours shall be; we shall have bodies in resurrection that are not subject to the laws that control us now.[62]

The bodies of the saints will be changed from corruptible flesh and blood, into incorruptible glorious and spiritual bodies suitable to the celestial world for eternal inheritance. The bodies of the believers will be similar to Christ's resurrected, glorified physical body. His redeemed people will receive spiritual and imperishable bodies to live with Christ forever.

Second Corinthians 3:18, NKJV, says, "But we all, with unveiled face, beholding as in a mirror the glory of the Lord, are being transformed into the same image from glory to glory, just as by the Spirit of the Lord." The Spirit enables believers to be like Christ. Hodge propounds,

> Conformity to Christ's likeness, since it arises from seeing his glory, must, of course, begin here. It is the vision of that glory, although only as in a mirror, that has transforming power. It is the vision of that glory, although only as in a mirror, that this has transforming power.[63]

Hodge points out that the glory of Christ is his divine excellence, hence the believer is enabled to see that Jesus is the Son of God. The believers shall be like Christ because they see him as is (1 John 3:2, NKJV). The believers shall conform to Christ's likeness. Paul reiterates, "And Just as we have borne the likeness of the earthly man, so shall we bear the likeness of

---

[62] Henry A. Ironside, *I and 2 Corinthians, An Ironside Expository Commentary* (Grand Rapids: Kregel, 2006), 283.
[63] Hodge, *2 Corinthians*, 67.

the man from heaven" (1 Cor 15:49, NIV). The bodies of Christians shall have a transformation that resembles Christ.

> This may mean the transformation proceeds from glory (that is, from the glory of Christ as apprehended by us) and results in glory. This explanation is adopted by the Greek Fathers. Or the expression indicates progression from one stag of glory to another. The transformation is carried forward without intermission, from the first scarcely discernible resemblance to full conformity to the likeness of Christ, both in soul and in body.[64]

The principles laid in 3:17, NKJV, are employed in 3:18 with the application of the spiritual transformation of believers.

In expounding 2 Corinthians 3:18, NKJV, Peter Naylor contends,

> Further, the intensification of their glory is spiritual, not facial and physical, their inner man "being transformed" into the "likeness" or image (Greek, eikon, whence the English 'icon'/ikon) of Christ. This comes about through the work of the 'Lord, the Spirit' who operates in the hearts of his people.[65]

The text explains that Christians behold the mirrored glory of the Lord, seeing and reflecting God through the image of God, the Lord Jesus Christ. It is important to understand that Paul in the text is expounding the concept that all believers will have the same bodies as Christ. Ralph Martin propounds, "The verb 'being transformed,' suggests a link with Christ, as God's 'image,' who is the prototype for all who belong to him and in whom he is taking shape (Gal 4:19)."[66] The believers shall take the form, shape, image and likeness of Christ because they will be with him for

---

[64] Ibid., 68.

[65] Peter Naylor, *A Study Commentary on 2 Corinthians* (Darlington, England: Evangelical, 2002), 164.

[66] Ralph P. Martin, *2 Corinthians*, Word Biblical Commentary, vol. 40, 2nd ed. (Grand Rapids: Zondervan, 2014), 215.

eternity. Their glorified bodies shall be in conformity with that of Christ to live in heaven with God, which will be a glorious day that everyone should wish for.

Colossians 3:10, NKJV, says, "And put on the new man, which is renewed in knowledge after the image of him that created him: The believers' position is acceptance in Christ, and they are granted spiritual power and regeneration. Moule writes, "By union with Him his members become repetitions of Him the glorious Archetype. . . So as to be like God, who created, constituted the new creation as He did the old."[67] The image of God consisted in man's resemblance to the moral attributes of God. Wilson explains,

> But the moral likeness to his all-glorious Maker was the principal part of man's honor. . .. So that knowledge, righteousness, true holiness, and a disposition to delight in all good works, constitute the main parts of the image of God in Adam was created; the dominion over the creature accompanying it.[68]

His restoration back to God is only possible through the sacrifice and mediation of Christ. Wilson puts an emphatic point in saying that the new man resembles, in some faint degree, the perfections of the Creator. He bears his image in his moral attributes as he exhibits a distant resemblance of righteousness, holiness, and beneficence.[69]

The image of putting away old nature and putting on new nature marks the transition from vices to virtues. After the renewal of all the vices in a person, virtues set in through the work of the Holy Spirit, thus renewing the image of God in believers. The new life in a believer begins to shape character, attitude, behavior, and lifestyle. The renewal of the inner being is not merited to any individual because their efforts; good works cannot please God because it is the work of the Holy Spirit. The passive voice shows that the result does not come from man's efforts or works, but the Holy Spirit sanctifies believers to be more like Christ. Christ came to

---

[67] Moule, *Studies in Colossians & Philemon*, 125

[68] Wilson, *Expository on Colossians*, 295.

[69] Wilson, *Expository on Colossians*, 298.

perfect other image-bearers to be more like Him. The believer becomes a new person, old things pass away—all things become new and the believer becomes the creative handiwork of God.

The next section discusses the consummation in which Christ establishes God's kingdom and the final completion of work perfecting image-bearers. Paul expounds on the consummation and Christ establishing God's kingdom forever.

Consummation

Jesus will return to establish God's kingdom completely. The kingdom of God will be established by Christ on His return. Christ inaugurated the kingdom of God in His death and resurrection. Although He is present today among His people, it is not in all his fullness. When He returns to earth at the appointed time, the Lord's righteous rule will be recognized by all creation, including His enemies under His feet (1 Cor 15:27-28, NKJV). When a Pharisee asked Jesus about the coming of the kingdom of God, Jesus answered, "The coming of the kingdom of God is not something that can be observed, nor people say, 'Here it is,' or 'There it is,' because the kingdom of God is in your midst," (Luke 17:20-21, NIV). The kingdom of God is partly present and partly future. The kingdom of God is a reality and is available now to overcome Satan and spiritual forces. Consummation is the coming together of everything that marks the completion, fulfillment, and realization of the kingdom of God when Christ returns for the second time.

Jesus' second coming has numerous interpretations in which the church has been divided by beliefs about his kingdom. Keith Bailey points out,

> The Second Coming of Jesus Christ is an article of faith among all who call themselves Christians, but beliefs about the details of His return and the relationship of His return to the kingdom of God divide the church into three major camps: the amillennialists, the postmillennialists, and the premillennialists. One of the key difference's centers on

interpretation of the thousand-year period mentioned in
Revelation 20.[70]

Amillennialists do not believe in the literal one-thousand-year reign of
Christ; instead, they interpret Revelation 20 as the church age at present.
The second group is postmillennialists, who believe that when the church
engages in aggressive evangelism and there is revival in the church, then
the kingdom of God will come, and after one thousand years of Christ's
blessings, Christ will return to establish His kingdom and the world
will end. The third group is premillennialists, who believe that Christ is
coming again and He will set up the kingdom of God. They believe in the
reality of the kingdom literally and that it will take place for the period of
one thousand years.

The first coming of Christ brought in moral, social, and spiritual
changes, and His second coming for the consummation of the kingdom
and judgment of all humankind will be new beginning for everything.
Christ's kingdom will be gracious, spiritual, and redemptive. Hodges
distinctively points,

> The kingdom of God is to be distinguished from the
> kingdom of heaven in five aspects: 1. The kingdom
> of God is universal, including all moral intelligences
> willingly subject to the will of God, whether angels, the
> Church, or saints of past or future dispensations, while
> the kingdom of heaven is Messianic, mediatorial, and
> Davidic, and has for its object the establishment of the
> kingdom of God in earth. 2. The kingdom of God is
> entered only by new birth; the kingdom of heaven, during
> this age, *is the sphere of profession which may be real or false.*
> 3. Since the kingdom of heaven is the earthly sphere of
> the universal kingdom of God, the two have almost all
> things in common. . . . 4. The kingdom of comes not with
> outward show; but is chiefly that which is inward and

---

[70] Keith M. Bailey, *Christ's Coming and His Kingdom* (Harrisburg, PA: Christian
Publications, 1981), 7.

spiritual; while the kingdom of heaven is organic, and is to be manifested in glory on earth. 5. The kingdom of heaven merges into the kingdom of God when Christ, having 'put all enemies under his feet,' shall have delivered up the kingdom to God, even the Father.[71]

The kingdom of God is consummated when Christ returns for the second time to establish God's kingdom. Hodge puts it into perspective with logical analysis. God's kingdom is for born-again Christians, who are the bride of Christ, the church. The qualification for the kingdom of God is the grace of God and redemption through repentance and forgiveness by Christ Jesus. Christians are then transformed into newness through the work of the Holy Spirit who sanctifies the believer into the image and likeness of God. The next section discusses Jesus completing his work of perfecting image-bearers.

Jesus will complete his work of perfecting image-bearers (1 Cor 1:8; Eph 1:4; Phil 1:9-11; Col 1:22; Rev 20:7-10, NKJV). "Who will also confirm you to the end, that you may be blameless in the day of our Lord Jesus" (1 Cor 1:8, NKJV). Mark Taylor writes,

> Paul expands on the thought of the Day of the Lord by affirming, "He will keep you strong to the end." The context, this confirmation is further explained as "blameless," that is, without accusation on the Day of the Lord. Colossians 1:22 provides further insight on Paul's meaning: "But now he has reconciled you by Christ's physical body through death to present you holy in his sight, without blemish and free from accusation."[72]

The image-bearers are being sanctified by the Holy Spirit—being perfected until the return of Christ when He will complete the work of perfecting them. Jay Adams asserts,

---

[71] Jesse Wilson Hodges, *Christ's Kingdom and Coming* (Grand Rapids: Wm. B. Eerdmans, 1957), 23.

[72] Mark Taylor, *1 Corinthians*, The New American Commentary, vol. 28 (Nashville: B & H, 2014), 45.

> In perfect, glorified bodies that are like the risen body of Jesus, we shall be able to appreciate and bask in the glory of God. Once cleansed and perfected, we will be able to approach the God who has always been unapproachable because of our infirmities and our sins. There, made perfectly holy, in perfect bodies, circumstances will be rapidly different.[73]

Adams points out that believers will have perfect bodies, like that of risen Christ with a glorified body.

Paul expounded the concept of a glorified body for all believers as Christ was after His resurrection. Paul then strikes a chord when he says they have been sanctified in Christ Jesus and are called to be holy. In Ephesians, Paul expounds that Christ will perfect image-bearers: "Just as He chose us in Him before the foundation of the world, that we should be holy and without blame before Him in love" (Eph. 1:4, NKJV). Paul discusses the fact that Christ chose His people before the foundation of the world, and in essence, in His sovereignty, grace, and love, Christ perfects and sanctifies His chosen people to be like Him. Andrew Lincoln asserts,

> In Eph 1:4 holiness, blamelessness, and love are complementary terms. On its negative side's holiness is the absence of moral defect or sin, i.e., blameless, while, on its positive sides, as moral perfection, it displays itself in love which is the fulfillment of God's will. In this reference a theocentric perspective predominates, for a life of holiness, blamelessness, and love has its source in and response to the gracious election of God and is lived 'before him,' that is, conscious that God's presence and God's approval are one's ultimate environment.[74]

Lincoln extends the horizon of God's foreknowledge about those He chose before the foundation of the world.

---

[73] Jay E. Adams, *Hope for the New Millenniums* (Woodruff, SC: Timeless Text, 1994), 15.
[74] Andrew T. Lincoln, *Ephesians*, Word Biblical Commentary, vol. 42 (Dallas: Word, 1990), 25.

According to Scripture, predestination is God's foreordaining what is going to pass in history. In His divine power, God prepares in advance and chooses beforehand what will take place; He has foreknowledge about the future. Harry Uprichard writes,

> If predestination is God's ordering of destiny, then *election is* God's choosing of persons. . . The New Testament continues and develops this theme of election as God's means of choosing sinner for salvations. Paul notes the purpose of election, which is with a view to holiness: "to be holy and blameless in his sight." Holiness is that moral purity and apartness of God which he bestows in salvation on the Christian.[75]

The doctrine of election is not dependent on human knowledge, efforts, or power, but is determined by God alone who is sovereign and omniscient. Some churches have over-emphasized or exaggerated the doctrine of election and predestination.

God's foreknowledge about the future is further discussed by Walter Taylor:

> The activity of God in blessing is further detailed by **chose** and **destined**. The verb **chose** is literally the word "elect"; the word **destined** is the Greek word for "foresaw." The electing activity of God is no late breaking development. It occurred before the world was created and it occurred in him, that is, in Christ. Likewise, in his love, God foresaw (**destined**) through Jesus Christ that the recipients would be God's children.[76]

God chose believers before the foundation of the world. He redeemed Christians and destined them to eternity without blemish.

---

[75] Harry Uprichard, *A Study Commentary on Ephesians* (Darlington, England: Evangelical, 2004), 34.

[76] Walter F. Taylor, *Ephesians*, Augsburg Commentary on the New Testament (Minneapolis: Augsburg, 1985), 34, emphasis original.

In Philippians 1:9, NKJV, Paul wrote that Christians' love should increase more in the knowledge of God. Todd Still asserts,

> The assembly is to be marked by purity as they await and anticipate the Parousia (on "day of Christ. To be sure, this level of moral excellence requires diligence and vigilance on the part of believers. In the spiritual striving, however, they are to be mindful that the fruit of righteousness they seek is available in and is attainable through Christ.[77]

For Paul, standing right with God, and right living before God, is a reflection of Christ's righteousness and God's glory. Paul specifically urges the Philippians to produce the "fruits" of righteousness. Gerald Hawthorne and Ralph Martin write,

> Paul makes it clear, however, that this crop of goodness is not self-generated, nor can it be. For the "fruits" he has in mind is supernatural and is produced through Jesus Christ. . . God is the ultimate finality of the Christian life, and as such he alone to be honored and praised by all.[78]

The Holy Spirit enables believers to live righteous lives and to produce fruits. Christ is perfecting image-bearers and will complete the work when He comes for the second time.

Colossians 1:22, NKJV, complements other texts that have been presented about how Christ will complete the work of perfecting the image-bearers. Robert Wall reiterates,

> Verses 13-14 help us understand what happens at the beginning of our spiritual journey, when we are converted to or confirmed in Christ for our salvation from darkness and death. Verses 15-20 celebrate Christ's current and

---

[77] Todd D. Still, *Philippians and Philemon*, Smyth and Helwys Bible Commentary (Macon, GA: Smyth and Helwys, 2011), 34.

[78] Gerald F. Hawthorne and Ralph P. Martin, *Philippians*, Word Biblical Commentary, vol. 43 (Nashville: Nelson Reference and Electronic, 2004),

cosmic lordship over God's creation and new creation, and show why we can be confident, even in the midst of a broken and fallen world. . . Finally, based on verses 12-23, we are drawn toward the future, we are drawn toward the future, the eternal consequences of our reconciliation with God through Christ.[79]

Christ is in the business of perfecting image-bearers, and the Holy Spirit guides believers to live holy and righteous lives in order to draw others to Christ as they reflect the glory of God. Living a righteous life is the work of the Holy Spirit living in Christians.

Nicholas Wright points out the fundamental reasons why the Colossians should exhibit the fruits of the Holy Spirit:

> Paul now applies verse 20 to the problem of verse 12, and concludes that God *has reconciled you by Christ's physical body through death to present you holy in his sight.* He does not say that God's action in Christ, and the Colossians' acceptance of the gospel, have automatically and instantly made them perfect. Having been given a new life, they must behave in accordance with it.[80]

Christ's purpose is to present Christians before God as holy in His sight and without blemish. The language in the quote is in accordance with the Jewish sacrificial ritual, which denoted sacrifice without blemish or defects. God creates a holy people in Christ. Wright continues,

> This he is doing in practice, by refashioning their lives according to the pattern of the perfect life, that of Christ. This he will do in the future, when that work is complete and the church enjoys fully that which at present it awaits in hope. The present process, which begins with patient

---

[79] Robert W. Wall, *Colossians and Philemon,* IVP New Testament, Commentary (Downer Groves, IL: IVP, 1993), 82.

[80] Nicholas T. Wright, *Colossians and Philemon*, Tyndale New Testament Commentaries, vol. 1 (Downers Grove, IL: IVP, 1986), 82.

> Christian living and ends with the resurrection itself, will
> result in Christians being presented without shame or fear
> before God, as glad subjects before their king.[81]

Christians are being molded in the image and likeness of Christ and being sanctified by the Holy Spirit, and Christ will complete the work of perfecting image-bearers at the proper time.

The book of Revelation contains apocalyptic literature that entails allegories and figures that need accurate interpretations. With special reference to Revelation 20:7-10, John writes the book with clarity of his vision from his imprisonment in the island of Patmos: "And when the thousand years expires, Satan shall be loosed out of his prison," (Rev. 20:7, KJV). The book of Revelation gives a detailed timeline of symbolic events. Parallel to the book of Revelation is the book of Daniel, which is also apocalyptic in nature, depicting the symbolic events at the end of the age. James Hamilton explains,

> Revelation presents Daniel's seventieth week as taking
> place between Christ's ascension and his return. At the
> end of Daniel's seventieth week, Christ comes in judgment
> and fights the Battle of Armageddon (16:12-16; 17:14;
> 19:19). At the conclusion of the battle, the beast and the
> false prophet are thrown into the lack of fire (19:20), and
> Satan will not join the lake of fire until the thousand years
> (20:20).[82]

From his visions, John writes the events as if he were seeing them happening. For a thousand years, Satan is not thrown into the lake of fire; instead, he is seized and bound and is thrown into Abbys, shut and sealed over him for a thousand years. The believers who remained faithful at the start of a thousand years are raised from the dead and will reign with Christ for a thousand years (20:4-6, KJV).

After a thousand years, Satan is then released and "And will go out to

---

[81] Wright, *Colossians and Philemon*, 83.
[82] James M. Hamilton, *Revelation: The Spirit Speaks to the Churches* (Wheaton, IL: Crossway, 2012), 376.

deceive the nations in the four corners of the earth-Gog, Magog, and to gather them for battle. In number they are like the sand on the seashore" (Rev. 20:8, NIV). John then writes about Satan being thrown into the lake of fire with false prophets: "The devil, who deceived them, was cast into the lake of fire and brimstone where the beast and false prophets are. And they will be tormented day and night forever and ever" (Rev. 20:10, NKJV). Hamilton asserts, "Amillenialists argue that the battle in (Rev. 20:7-10, NKJV) is another description of the battle in (Rev. 19:17-21, NKJV), but the details are simply too different for that to be the case."[83] Satan and the false prophets are neither pardoned nor annihilated. In Revelation 20:7-10, NKJV, John writes about the final battle at the end of the millennium. John does not tell why Satan is being let loose. Mitchell Reddish writes,

> In a typical apocalyptic understanding, all that happens occurs within the ultimate purposes of God. Even the lease of Satan is John's way of emphasizing the formidable power of evil. Even when it appears that the evil has been contained and is no longer a threat, it has the capacity to rebound and wreak havoc in one's life.[84]

As John writes, Gog and Magog symbolize those nations that are deceived by Satan and those whom God will destroy. God will be declared the supreme ruler.

According to Reddish, John borrowed the Gog and Magog tradition:

> Whereas in Ezekiel, Gog is a person and Magog is the land over which he rules, in Revelation both Gog and Magog have become the names of evil nations. In Ezekiel, even though Gog has taken on mythical proportions, he is still a localized threat, the foe from the North. In Revelation, Gog and Magog are all-embracing symbols

---

[83] Hamilton, *Revelation*, 377.

[84] Mitchell G. Reddish, *Revelation*, Smyth and Helwys Bible Commentary (Macon, GA: Smyth and Helwys, 2001), 385.

for all the nations or peoples who are in rebellion against God.[85]

God finally defeats Satan and Satan's doom is at the conclusion of the millennium. Lamar Cooper presents three interesting arguments, which are summarized by Paige Patterson:

> Lamar Cooper, in the New American Commentary volume in Ezekiel, chronicles seven possible interpretations of the battle but finds in the end three major possibilities. The first is the Gog and Magog actually refers to the same battle by that name in Revelation 20. The second views the battle as Armageddon at the close of the tribulation period, chronicled at the end of chap. 16. The third view is a combination of the first two, including that this final conflict of history occurs at two different times with an interim period of 1,0000 years.[86]

Gog and Magog represent false prophets who have been deceived by Satan to perpetuate his deception. The devil has deceived many people and, together with his false prophets, will be thrown into the lake of fire where they belong and God will summon them for eternal punishment.

All the enemies of God—Satan, false prophets, and those who chose not to serve God—will be thrown in the lake of fire for eternity. Patterson writes, "Apparently part of what it means to be made in the image of God is to have indestructibility or immortality as part of what it means to be a spiritual being. A choice is to be made as to whether one wishes to be associated with God or to be left his own prowess."[87] It is imperative to understand that, in the New Testament, hell was not originally made for human beings, but it was made for Satan and his angels (Matt 25:41, NKJV). However, the lake of burning fire with sulfur, *Gehenna*, is the place for Satan with his angels and those who reject Christ. The devil and

---

[85] Ibid., 386.

[86] Paige Patterson, *Revelation*, The New American Commentary, vol. 39 (Nashville: B & H, 2012), 356.

[87] Ibid., 358.

his angels will experience excruciating torment for eternity. Christ will then usher in a new heaven and new earth where the perfected image-bearers will abide with Christ forever. Eternity for the righteous and holy, perfected by Christ, will inherit and live-in harmony forever with the Lamb, Christ Jesus.

The *imago Dei* in humanity makes humans unique and different from other animals. God created man in His own image and likeness to display His glory on earth through humanity. After the fall, the image and likeness of God in man were impaired and distorted. However, some imprints of God's image and likeness in man remain because God did not reduce man to the level of animals. God restores His image and likeness in man through His Son, Jesus Christ, the perfect image-bearer. Other image-bearers have been redeemed through the death and the resurrection of Christ. God's image-bearers have been redeemed to proclaim and share God's love. The next chapter lays out a teaching series that will help Christians in Zimbabwe to proclaim and share God's love by living out the Great Commission with people with HIV/AIDS.

Family Values and Morals

Family values connects the family to each other, community, society, nation and the world as one big family. Family values are fundamental into shaping the children's future. The family values and morals are the beliefs that the family upholds as right or wrong, good or bad, and ethical compass that direct and guide the family members wherever they are in the world. It is the understanding that man is created equal and have the same rights regardless of race, color, ethnicity or creed. All human beings deserve to be honored, respected, dignity, humility and kindness. It also includes hard working, compassion, responsibility, creativity, honesty, polite, justice, fairness and integrity. The verse, "Train a child in the way he should go, and when he old he will not turn from it," (Proverbs 22:6, NIV). Children can be spoiled and be cultivated to be disobedient. If the child cannot respect, honor and be obedient to his/her parents, he will not respect, honor or be obedient to his/her teacher, coach or anyone who is above him/her. The reasonable service, (*Diakonia*, Greek), to serve which is spiritual worship.

Christian values are embedded in Christ's character, attributes, virtues and compassion.

Paul discusses, "But the fruit of the Spirit is love, joy, peace, patience, kindness, faithfulness, gentleness, goodness and self-control. Against such things, there is no law," (Galatians 5:22, NKJV). The fruit is the result of bearing and the fruit produces because it in the tree and branches. A fruit to grow needs to abide in the tree. Christ is the vine and Christians are the branches and Christians must produce the fruits and they are known to be Christ's disciples by their fruits. "By their fruit you will recognize them. Do people pick up grapes from thorn bushes, or figs from thistles?" (Matt. 7:16, NIV). The vine and the branches in John 15, illustrates that the tree produces the same fruits of the same kind. Children who come from a descent and godly family can be easily be recognized where they belong. A good tree produces a good fruit. Godly parenting is the foundational and the source of instilling moral and godly values to children.

There are some insightful values that the children from their parents to have lasting impact in their life's things such as touch. Children love to be touched appropriately and meaningfully touch from their parents. Touch communicates deep relationship and mutual love between parents and children. Spoken words, speak volumes in assuring children and approval. Negative words discourage children to share their views, aspirations and vision in life. Affirmation to your children activate confident, courage, inspiration and aspirations to excel in their dreams and reach their God given potentials. Parents should be actively committed to their children's home, sports, clubs, and games. Forgiveness is pivotal in developing and cultivating good rapport with your children. Children make mistakes all the time and parents should extend an olive branch of forgiving and reconciling with their children after correcting them in love. Pray with your children, do Bible studies and devotions with them, fellowship at home and with their friends. Pray for their studies, life partners, their carriers, and friends. Spent time with them and be involved in their activities. The family that prays together, sticks together and achieve much together.

CHAPTER TWO
THE BLOSSOM OF FAMILY

Family Worship

Family worship is the epicenter of the family's survival and longevity. What is worship?

Worship is to honor, worthiness, venerate someone or being. The Old Testament Hebrew word, *Shachah* means to bow down. According to Strong Concordance, *Shachal* means "to bow down" or "worship." Family worship is when the parents and children come together to worship the Father, giving Him honor, praises, singing and hailing His Name. Worship is reverence offered to a divine being who is supernatural or directed to deity. It is the time to fellowship with one another and God Himself. King David wrote Psalms of praises and worship of the living God such as "Search me, God, and know my heart; test and know me and my anxious thoughts," (Psalm 139:23-24, NIV), "Praise the Lord, on my soul; all my inmost being, praise his holy name," (Psalm 103:1, NIV), "Oh give thanks to the Lord, call upon His Name; Make known His deeds among the peoples," (Psalm 105:1, NKJV).

Family worship can be fun when each members of the family rotate in sharing the devotions for each day with the father summarizing the Scripture of the day and the making application as the head of the house. The family members can take time to pray for each member of the family, extended family, neighbors, friends, the city or the town and the nation as stipulated by Apostle Paul to pray for the nations (Romans 13:1-7, NKJV). The family worship can include singing using the music instruments, such as guitars, key boards and tambourines, harps, "Shout for joy to the Lord, all the earth, burst into jubilant song with music; make music to the Lord with harp, with the harp and the sound of singing, with trumpets and the blast of the ram's horn-shout for joy before the Lord King," (Psalm 98:4-6, NIV). Family worship is the heartbeat and the alter to submit petitions to God for others and the family. Coming to the table as a family to worship God is the most-sweetest moments of the family.

However, cultures, traditions and customs are different from country to country. In a culture I grew up, the Ndebele culture, the father was a figure head that no mutual relationship with the children. They were always a house or hut for the father. He would not interact with the children so fluidly. Children were having their huts where they played far from the father. When it was a time for lunch or dinner, the father would be served his food in his house or hut, alone far from children. The father was a figure venerated, feared and not easy to approach. If you needed something from the father, there was a protocol in which you start to approach your mother and tell her what you wanted from your father. Then the mother would reach out to the father with high respect and dignity to present your request. So many African cultures and traditions have similar structures but depending on each culture and tradition. In that context children to sit together with the father and mother on the same table was like a taboo. However, times have changed and culture and traditions have revolved and the modern families, have adopted the western civilization and African culture and tradition are now similar to those of the West. In the same veins, they are cultures and traditions that are still following the old tradition and culture. In that context, family worship the set up would be different and varied.

The conflict of Christianity versus cultural and traditional rituals. Many families are caught in between and get confused to choose either Christianity moral values or cultural and traditional norms for their children. John S. Mbiti, one the African Theologian asserts, "The youth are ritually introduced to the art of communal living. This happens when they withdraw from other people to live alone in the forest or in a specifically prepared huts away from the villages. They go through a period of withdrawal from society, absent from home, during which time they receive secret instruction before they are allowed to rejoin their relatives at home."[88] Family worship and cultural norms conflict in this context. That's why syncretism comes into play in which Christians live mixed lives of Christian lifestyle and mix it with traditional and cultural norms.

"The word syncretism was first used by Plutarch in a political sense to show a united front against a common enemy, *synkretismos*. In the sixteenth century, the word was used to describe Bessarion's attempt to reconcile Plato and Aristotle. During the Reformation, the word retained its original political meaning in spite of profound differences, to combine forces against a common foe. Syncretism is defined as a systematic attempt to combine, blend and reconcile and inharmonious often conflicting religious elements."[89]

Syncretism is the problem of religious pluralism. There is a need for theological reconstruction:

> We should not focus on extracting principles from the Bible and applying these to culture. Scripture is not a book existing independent of us. Scripture is the living testimony to what God has done and continues to do, and we are part of that testimony.... The application of Scripture is a gradual process of coming together, of life touching life. Our particular culture encounters the activity of God in building up a community of His people throughout history, a community that now includes us and our particular traditions, history and culture.[90]

Christianity is above culture because it is the way of life. God is aware of every culture and tradition of every society, and that's the reason he planted them in that geographical location and allowed them to live as

---

[88] John S. Mbiti, African Religions and Philosophy, 2nd Edition, (Oxford: Heineman, 1969), 118.

[89] Wilbur O'Donovan, *Biblical Christianity in Modern Africa* (Carlisle: Paternoster Press, 2000), 263.

[90] Tokunboh, Adeyemo et al, *African Bible Commentary* (Nairobi: World Alive Publishers, 2006), 4.

they but he does not condone the worship of other gods, idols, objects, mountain, trees, animals, birds or reptiles. He has revealed Himself through general revelation in which the universe, the expanse of the galaxy, and all visible things to display his majesty and power. "In the past God overlooked such ignorance, but now he commands all people everywhere to repent. For he has set a day when he will judge the world with justice by the man he has appointed. He has given proof of this to everyone by raising him from the dead," (Acts 17:30, NIV). Family worship is central to all Christian families as the family alter brings the family together, glued to their Christian values and mandate regardless of cultural and traditional backgrounds. It is God ordained and God centered. Joshua was instructed to meditate on the word of God day and night, not to turn to the right or to the left and not to depart from your mouth. The children of Israelites were instructed to teach the word of God to their children.

God's Family Business

When a person repents and confess that Jesus is Lord and believe that Jesus Christ and died and rose from the dead on the third day, will be saved and adopted into the family of God. Paul wrote, "That if you confess with your mouth, 'Jesus is Lord 'and believe in your heart that God raised him from the dead, you will be save. For it is with your heart that you believe and are justified, and it is with your mouth that you confess and are saved.," (Romans 10:9-10, NKJV). When you become part of God's family, you become the heir and your Father's business becomes your business. A family by definition is a group of one or more parents and their children, related by blood or marriage. That's a sociology definition. There is a father and a mother, children or relatives.

> In God's economy, believers are a family of God and Christ is the Head of the church. We are all related through the blood of Jesus. We are God's family. God has a business of reaching out to the lost sons and daughters, like the prodigal son in (Luke 15:11-32, NKJV). God wants us to bring them back into His kingdom.

God's Family Business is the mindset of God to work with us as family members. The goal of God is to bring them all back into the kingdom and does not want them to perish, "The Lord does not delay his promise, as some understand delay, but he is patient with you not wanting any to perish but wants everyone to repent," (II Peter 3:9, CSB). They are 7.5 billion in the world, according to the population census in 2018. There are about 2.3 billion Christians in the world according to Pew Research Center, in 2015.

God has been partners with humanity right from the very beginning God Entrusted Human beings

1. Adam and Eve: God Instructed them, "To Be fruitful and multiply and fill the earth and subdue it…" (Gen. 1:28, NKJV).

2. He communicated his word with men and led them to write down His word for permanent preservation. He superintendent in writing the Holy Scriptures and inspired them with the Holy Spirit (I Cor. 2:13, NKJV)

3. He worked with the prophets to proclaim his oracles, judgment, and grace "Knowing this first, that no prophecy of Scripture is of private interpretation, for prophecy never came by the will of man, but holy men of God spoke as they were moved by the Holy Spirit," (II Peter 1:20-21, NKJV).

4. Christ was born of a woman, Mary, through virgin birth, "But when the set time (*Kairos*) had fully come, God sent his Son, born of a woman, born under the law," (Gal.4:4, NKJV). God allowed human beings to participate, and used the woman's womb to bring the Son of God into the world for their salvation.

5. When king Herod was jealous and wanted to kill Jesus the King who was born in Bethlehem, Mary and Joseph were instructed by the angel to escape to Egypt for refuge for three years until king Herod died (Matt. 2:1-15, NKJV). Egypt had been a traditional place for refuge for Jews in Biblical times (I Kings 11:40; Jer. 26:21, NKJV).

6. On the way to the cross, Simon of Cyrene assisted Christ to carry the cross to Calvary, (Matt. 27:32, NKJV).

7. When Jesus breathed His last and died, one of His disciples, Joseph of Arimathea and Nikodemus asked His body and buried him in Joseph's own private tomb, (Mark 15:43, 46, NKJV).

8. Jesus entrusted the Gospel to the twelve disciples, to the seventy-two and hundred and twenty. "But you will receive the power when you the Holy Spirit comes on you; and will be my witnesses in Jerusalem, and in Judea, and in Samaria, and to the ends of the end of the earth," (Acts 1:8, NIV). See where we are today.

9. "Go therefore and make disciples of all nations, baptizing them in the name of the Father, of the Son and of the Holy Spirit, and teaching them to obey everything I have commanded you...," (Matt.28:18-20, CSB).

10. "Watch and pray so that you will not enter into temptation," (Matt. 26:41, NIV).

The Commission of Believers (II Timothy 3: 16-17, NKJV)

"All Scripture is God breathed" The very words originally given by God to men were God breathed. The Word of God is profitable:

1. The Bible is Profitable for Doctrine/Teaching. It sets the mind of God to such teachings as Trinity, angels, man, sin, salvation, sanctification, the church and eschatology (future events).

2. It is profitable for reproof, to point out things that are displeasing to God from us

3. It is profitable to refute errors, (Gnosticism in the first & second centuries, hence the epistles John, Peter, Jude, Pauline Epistles. Today false prophets and teachers still emerge today.

4. It is profitable for corruption, pointing out things that are not right to correct and to have sound minds and to fear God.

5. It is profitable for instruction in righteousness. The grace of God compels us to live godly lives.

6. It is profitable to make a believer complete and mature in Christ through the power of the Holy Spirit and the Word of God

7. It is profitable to equip and to bring forth every good work in contrast to the worldly standard which requires academic degrees to be equipped for life. In God's Kingdom, you come as you are.

8. The Word is seasoned and sufficient for all our daily life. The just shall live by faith (Habakkuk 2:4, NKJV)

9. It is profitable because it has a full package for life: Grace, Faith, Salvation, Security and eternity.

10. It is profitable because it preserves my life on earth and for eternity. The seal of the Spirit is on us to be his own (Eph. 1:8, NKJV). No one can snatch us from His gracious hands and "even the gates of hell shall not prevail against the chosen one (Matt. 16:17-19, NKJV).

11. You are loved by God and you are the apple of His eye. "The eyes of the Lord are on the righteous, and his ears are open to their cry for help," (Psalm 34:15, NIV).

12. Paul makes a conclusion and declaration in (Romans 8:35-39, NIV) "Who shall separate us from the Love of Christ? Shall tribulation, or stress, or nakedness, or peril, or sword…" "For I am persuaded that neither death nor life, nor angels, nor principalities nor powers, no things present nor things to come, nor any other created thing, shall be able to separate us from the love of God which is in Christ Jesus our Lord."

When a believer becomes a child and family member of God, Christ teaches him/her to be Christ-minded and to engage in God's business. Christ says, "Come ye after me, and I will make you fishers of men." (Matthew 4:19, ASV).

1. Come (Verb), (Greek= ***Erchomai***) means to "to start" and "to set out" referring to a journey and to arrive at a place. It actually means relocate your space and go to Jesus's space. Move from where you are and move to the One calling you.

It actually means Christ cannot deal with you where you are. You need to move away from where you are and go closer to Him so that He will show you where to go. Come out from your cocoon and your comfort zone. Christ is faithful and trustworthy to go to Him, relocate from your space, your environment, and be with Him.

2. Follow Me (Verb), ***Oikonomos***, to follow, ***akolouthos*** a follower which denotes union, likeness. ***Katakoloutheo*** - follow after, follow behind.

Parakoloutheo - to follow close up, or side by side, to conform to. Do not follow people that you don't even know their characters or their hidden lives.

3. **Make you** - (Verb), ***Eleutheroo*** - set free, release from bandage, to remove the restrictions of sin (darkness). Being delivered by God into true spiritual liberty (growth).

4. **Fishers of Men** - (Verb), First, Greek word, *"anthropos"* meaning "men". Fishers were those who caught fish for commercial purposes as a trade. This refers to the whole business of fishing, the techniques, skills, marketing the fish. Jesus was telling Andrew and Peter to follow the true Messiah and that they were participants.

With that background of Jesus calling out the disciples, it was the second time that Jesus called Peter and Andrew.

> In (John 1:35-42, NKJV), they were called to salvation in Judea and now they are called to service in Galilee. Peter and Andrew were fishermen but Jesus called them to be fishers of men, same analogy of fishing business but now different trade of fishing *anthropos*, men, human beings. Different makeup of the products. Fish, very quickly rot when caught. Men, are very quick to dessert, to quit or to stray.

In God's economy and in God's business one's responsibility is to **follow** Christ. Christ's responsibility to empower the believers to be successful fishermen. Following Jesus involves **imitation** of His **character**, the ministry character and His ways of doing things. What is more important in God's business is to obey Him, "To do what is right and just is more acceptable to the Lord than sacrifice," (Proverbs 21:3, NIV). Don't substitute your eloquence, personality and wisdom for true spirituality. Do not sugarcoat yourself to serve in the sanctuary. God loves you as you are. Endure discomfort but be patient, resilient, live by faith, follow Christ, and focus on Christ alone.

Children a Heritage & Blessings

(Biblical Sociology)
Ephesians 5, Biblical roles of the husband and wife.

God has given a model of a family, the husband and the head of the family and the wife as a helper. Paul addresses how the couple should understand their responsibility towards one another and God. In Ephesians 5: 22-24, NKJV, he first addresses the wife that she must submit to her husband as to the Lord. Basically, the way she submits to God in the way she must submit to her husband. Giving all her respect and reverence to her husband as if she is giving to the Lord as an honor to her husband. As Christ is the head of the church, so her husband is the head of the household. As the church submits to Christ, so the wife should submit to her husband. This an appeal for personal piety in the Christian households. It must be understood in the context that it is the will of God. These forms of authority are in line with God's will to maintain order. Authority and submission are the pillars of any governing body, in the family, and the nation. The society must have an order, the household must have order. There is submission in the Godhead. "But I want you to know that the head of every man is Christ, the head of women is man, and the head of Christ is God," (I Cor.11:3, NKJV). It also must be clear that submission does not imply inferiority. Christ submits to God the father but it does imply that Christ is inferior to God the Father. The wife should understand that it is God's command. This submission only applies to their own husbands, not other men. By submitting to the authority of her husband, she is also submitting to the authority of Christ. This is a leadership pattern. This is the role of a woman that God gave her to submit husband.

In Ephesians 5:25, NKJV, Paul addresses the husband. The husband is the head of the household. God's command to the husband is to love his wife, just as Christ loved the church and gave himself up to her. The type of love employed here is the Greek word, (*agape*) which means sacrificial love. Christ sacrificed his life for all believers, the church. As Christ is the head of the church, so the husband is the head of the household. The same principle of Christ being the head of the church, so the husband is the head of the household. Christ loves the church so dearly that he shed his own blood for the church. The husband should love and sacrifice his life for his wife. The husband is the head of the wife and he has to love her. The manifestation of his love for her to provide for her, protect her, guide her, care for her, and provide a home for her. As Christ treats the church with respect and dignity, so does the husband treat his wife. The husband must love his wife as he loves his wife.

Ephesians 6:1-4 and Colossians 3:20-21 (NKJV), Biblical responsibilities of the parents and children.

The Biblical responsibility of the parents to the children to raise them in a Godly manner. The children must willingly submit to the authority of their parents. The duty of children is to submit and to obey their parents in the Lord because it is right. The parent-child relationship must be honored because it was ordained by God. They must obey in the Lord whether your parents are Christians or not. Their attitude to obey their parents is in line with God's will and is like obeying the Lord. The children's obedience to their parents should be as if it is to God. The obedience to their parents should be unconditional, in all matters except if it goes contrary to God's word and according to the will of God. However, if the parents force them to sin or do things that are contrary to the will of God, they should reject and comply with the demand. Firstly, obeying the parents is right, secondly, it is Scriptural. "Honor your father and your mother," (Exodus 20:12; Deut. 12:12, NKJV). The command has some blessings that they live long in this world. Children should honor, respect, love and care for their parents. Thirdly, their obedience to their parents will yield in that it may be well with them. The fourth benefit is that they have a full and long life. Filial obedience results in longevity.

There is a warning to the fathers in verse 4, that the fathers should not exasperate their children; instead, they should bring them up in the training and instruction of the Lord. The advice is to avoid provoking their children to anger with unreasonable demands or expectations. This included nagging, harassment, being harsh to them unnecessarily. The children are to be loved, cared for under training with discipline, admonition, rebuke, reproof, warning but gentleness, tender hearted, loving and humility. Children are a blessing from the Lord (Psalm 127:3-5, NKJV).

Deuteronomy 6:4-6, NKJV, is in fact warnings against disobedience. When the Israelites would enter the Promised Land, God them to be in a right moral condition and not to forget who God is to them. God instructed Moses to tell the Israelites to be obedient to His statutes if they were to enjoy Canaan and they were to bear testimony to the truth that only God was the true God. They were to "You shall love the Lord your God with all your heart, and with all soul and with all your strength," (Deut. 6:5, NKJV). Further, they were instructed to teach and instruct their children diligently, passionately, and carefully to be obedient too to God. They should teach, guide and transfer the faith to their children. The commandments are to be to their hearts, both the parents and their children. They were to impress them on their children. They are four things they should do in order to impress God's law on their children. They should talk about the commandments to their children:

1. when they **sit** down with them at home
2. When they **walk** along the road
3. When they **lie down/sleep**
4. When they **wake up/get up**

To show the importance of God's law and the obedience to it, parents were instructed to tie them on their hands and on their foreheads as symbols. They were to write them on the doorframes of their houses and on their gates. This meant that their hands, eyes and mind were to be controlled by God's law.

Deut. 6:4-9, NKJV, Hear, in Hebrew, *"Shema"* were recited every day as a creed by devout Jews along with Deut.11:13-21, NKJV and also Numbers 15:37-41, NKJV. The children were to imitate their parents and to learn from their parents so that they would be a continuation of their devoutness to God and to His faithfulness from generation to generation.

Parents are to instill faith to their children by living and being good examples in their daily lives. It is imperative for the parents to have a family altar in which parents read, mediate and apply the Scriptures on their children. Daily devotions, prayer, Bible study, and discipleship of the children must be an intentional plan for every Christian family. Parents should create time to walk, exercise, read, and have fun with their children to have a bond and develop relationships. In doing so, they are able to share their faith, testimonies and experiences with their children. Parents are to share the Word of God with their children when they go to bed, and when they wake up in the morning.

Ephesians 6:1-4, NIV), Paul instructs the relationship between the parents and children. "Children, obey your parents in the Lode, for this is right. Honor your fathers and mother-which is the first commandment with a promise-that it may go well with you and that you may enjoy a long life on the earth. Fathers, do not exasperate your children; bring them up in the training and instruction of the Lord." If children are trained and instructed to fear the Lord, children are also trained and taught to obey and trust God.

Career Guidance

The parents have the responsibility to guide their children for their aspirations in life. The children have their wishes, aspirations, passions and carriers they want to pursue when they are out of colleges or universities. Help them to discover their own strengths and passions. If the parents are not the mentors, help them to find their own mentor to help them to go through their exploration of life. However, parents are there to guide them, counsel them and show the pros and cons, advantages and disadvantages, dangers, good and paying jobs. But at the end of the day, it is the children who have the ultimate decision to follow their dreams, passions and aspirations. The parents should subport their children. The parents have to speak their language and encourage them to aim high with their passions. Let them choose what they want to do but guide them through. Don't push for your own extension in order to fulfill your dreams that you failed to achieve in your life time. Le them chase their dreams without interference from the parents. You had your time and this is their own time too.

Guide in the direction of the Lord and to seek His counsel, "Trust in the Lord with all your heart and lean not on your own understanding; in all your ways, submit to him and he will make your paths straight," (Proverbs 3:5, NIV). The children have to be on person learning. Encourage them to volunteer, to shadow a professional, attend camps, internships, attend seminars and to get involved in the church. Parents should teach them to have good habits, good attitudes, good characters, good aptitude, respect, acknowledgement, appreciation, gratitude and to show love all the time.

CHAPTER THREE
PARENTS & CHILDREN IN DIASPORA

Parents Disconnect with Children

There is generation "Gap" between parents and children. The generation gap is a normal norm between parents and their children. It is a deniable fact and normal because the gap means there are years of differences between the two generations. This is a perception that has divided the families, the parents and their children. It could be thought to be a psychological or emotional contract, but it is a reality because the two were not born at the same time, the same environment, the geographical or scientific times. The fashion during which the parents lived and that of that of their children are different. The technological advancements and innovations, the society, education opportunities, the thinking patterns during which the parents were raised is different from their children. The technological advancements such as vehicles, planes, phones, computer science, industry, satellite. The societies, the economy, social mobility, lifestyle diet and early maturity because of food and diet are all different from generation to generation. The culture s and traditions are different and the worldviews are different, the racial segregations, gender equality, climate change influence behaviors. The generation gap plays a pivotal role as to the way we perceive the world and the way communication has changed over time.

The way the parents and their children access information are different.

The diseases, medicine, infrastructure, research, immigration with the concept of global village where the world in the finger-tips of many is evident of the generation gap, education online versus physical learning has changed dramatically. The internet has changed, with social media such as Instagram, Twitter, Facebook, YouTube, Spotify, Tik-Tok, Emails, Texting, Faxing etc.

Children anticipate love from their parents. They hunger for parent's approval. Children need the blessings from their parents.

a. **Touch**- Children love the meaningful touch from their parents

b. **Spoken words**- Children long for encouragements and approval. Negative words break the soft bones

c. **Vision**- Help your children to shape their future

d. **Active commitment**- Be committed to their home-work, activities at school, church and with their friends. Be there for them.

e. **Forgiveness**- Children make mistakes. Extend a word of reconciliation after correction.

f. **Pray**- Pray with them for their studies, life, future spouses, carriers, friends and pray as a family

g. **Communication**- open an environment of easy communication for their joy, worries and needs

h. **Time**- Spend time with them in whatever activities they are involved in. Spend quality time with your children and wife/husband.

i. The family that prays together sticks together and achieve much together.

j. "Children obey your parents in the Lord, for this is right. Honor your father and mother that it may go well with you and that you may live long in the land. Fathers do not provoke your children to anger, but bring them up in the discipline and instruction of the Lord" (Eph.6:1-4, NIV).

The children living with their parents in diaspora, having been brought when they were young has even widen the generation gap. The parents who were born and lived in their native countries and brought their children with them for work or education overseas. This doesn't matter whether missionary children overseas in Africa, Europe, Asia, North America, Australia or Latin America. Children are the same. The parents lived their lives, youth and adulthood in the native countries and they brought with their cultures, traditions, diet, taste, lifestyles, fashion, and of course, the concept of the family. It takes time to adapt and to adjust to a new culture environment, climate, the type food and the diet, taste, lifestyle, fashion in a new country. While the parents bring with them cultural and traditional residues from your native countries, they struggle to fully assimilate into a culture and the norms of the new country, it is opposite to children. The children easily adapt and assimilate into a new culture without much difficult in any given country.

The tag of cultural and traditional wars begins between parents and children. The children start to talk and speak the same language of the indigenous people and easily adapt and sail with the flow of a new culture, fashion, and they become part of the new normal. In the same vein, the parents want to continue to hang on their cultures and traditions, resisting the changes to adapt to a new normal. They fight with their children against assimilating in the new culture, insisting that they will misbehave and adopt the bad culture. The parents always think that their cultures and traditions are the best than any other cultures and traditions when it comes cultural, ethical, and moral values. They still insist to raise their as they were raised. Eventually, they discover that they can no longer force their children to do the chores, the duties, the manage their behaviors and to mold their characters the same their parents used to do. The family members are in constant conflicts and arguments in their daily lives. That's when the Biblical standard and Christian principles need to kick in such as (Ephesians 6:1-4, NIV). "Children, obey your parents in the Lord, for this is right. Honor your father and mother- which is the fir commandment with a promise-so that it may be well with you and enjoy long life on the earth. Fathers, do not exasperate your children; instead, bring them up in the training and instruction of the Lord). Both children are given instructions as to how they should relate and honor each other's spaces and knowing their boundaries. Mutual respect and honor are spelled out in these verses. Human rights apply to both the children and the parents.

The children of missionaries most of them are home schooled because the parents do not want their children to adopt the indigenous cultures and traditions. They want their children to be unique and stand out. They caution their children not to play with other children of a different race. They live a different than the indigenous people. It is as if they dropped with parachute in the middle of nowhere in the jungle and bring their cultures, tradition, customs, type of foods, diet, and many other baggage with them in order to live their lives as before, yet they call themselves missionaries. Some missionary parents discourage their children to learn the indigenous language. Such missionaries do not understand what they represent. As ambassadors of Christ, missionaries are supposed to be part of the community they are serving. They are to eat the same food of the people they are serving with, send their children to school where the indigenous children attend, educate and encourage their children to speak the same language the indigenous children speak. They represent Christ who became man, through incarnation and became Emmanuel, God with us. Can you imagine if Christ came down from heaven with His glory and lived a heavenly life not an earthly life with humanity? He was not going to be our Savior or Lord. "In the beginning was the Word, and the Word was with God and the Word was God...The Word became flesh and made his dwelling among us. We have seen his glory, the glory of the one only Son, who came from the Father, full of grace and truth," (John 1:1, 14, NIV). Christ became part of us, ate what we eat, wore what we wear, used the same mode of transport we used, learned in the same schools we learned, received the same education we received hence the incarnation model the missionaries should adopt.

Both children and parents may suffer mental disorders because of the restrained relationships. Parents should be aware of the symptoms in their children's lives and address them immediately when they notice the symptoms for the children's mental health. They following are some the mental disorders that can affect the children for long time they are not address through Biblical Counseling.

Bipolar

Bipolar is a disorder associated with episodes of mood swings of depression from low to manic high. Although the cause of bipolar is unknown but the environment and altered brain structure and chemistry can have great impact on an individual's behavior. The symptoms of bipolar are high or low energy, no motivation, not interest in daily activities, or insomnia. Jay Adam asserts, "In the downward cycling the depression certainly contributes to further failures as it often becomes the excuse for a faulty handling of sin itself. But, in contrast to those who would speak of changing the feelings in order to change the behavior, God reverses the order..."[91] The word of God is sufficient to counsel someone with bipolar disorder.

The Lord has ways to counsel people with bipolar disorders. Although this passage is not directly directed to bipolar disorder, king Saul of Israel had a spirit that bothered him all the time and God had a solution to soothe him through David. "And it came to pass, when the evil spirit from God was upon Saul, that David took the harp, and played with his hand: So, Saul was refreshed, and was well, and the evil spirit departed from him," (I Samuel 16:14-23, ASV). For those who have insomnia, the Palmist concludes, "It is in vain you for you to rise early, to sit up late, to eat the bread of sorrow: for so he giveth his beloved sleep," (Psalm 127:2b, KJV). This is not a direct rebuke to people but this shows that God is concerned about one to sleep well and that He grants sleep to those he loves. Some of the verses about those who are depressed and God delivers them. "The righteous cry out, and the Lord hears them; he delivers them from all their troubles. The Lord is close to the broken-hearted and saves those who are crushed in spirit. The righteous person may have many troubles, but the Lord delivers him from them all," (Psalm 34:17-19, NKJV); "Why, my soul, are you downcast? Why so disturbed within me? Put your hope in God, for I will yet praise him, my Savior and my God," (Psalm 42:11, NIV); "But those who hope in the Lord will renew their strength. They will soar on wings like eagles; they will run and not weary, they will walk and not be faint" (Isaiah 40;31, NIV).

Codependent

A codependent is anyone who cannot function independently on his own. His/her thinking and behavior is organized around someone or substance. He/she puts more priority to others than himself/herself. He/she is a people pleaser and can plan his/her activity around pleasing an individual

---

[91] Jay E. Adams, *Hope for the New Millenniums* (Woodruff, SC: Timeless Text, 1994), 15.

and trying to meet the needs of someone. Codependent is defined as, "Codependency refers to a mental, emotional, physical, and/or spiritual reliance on a partner, friend, or family member... Codependency is not a clinical diagnosis or a formally categorized personal disorder on its own. Generally speaking, codependency incorporates aspects of attachment style patterns developed in early childhood, and it can also overlap with other personality disorders, including dependent personality disorder."[92] (https://docs.google.com/document/d/1ORRkug4KmbcJq6wsiMkuZoe 2wJGLNy4ESvnVjjfXsJc/edit, Accessed February 2, 2021). This kind of person depends and relies on someone for his/her welfare. As stipulated, it is not a clinical diagnosis but an individual can attach to someone although it can be associated with disorder. It is due to a poor concept of self and poor boundaries that one fails to limit.

The Bible is very clear in that kind of pattern that one has to depend and rely on God alone not any individual or substance. One can have a friend, a family member or a partner but to depend and rely on them for one's survival, it is not approved in the Scripture except if someone has a special need. 'Even while we were still with you there with you, we gave you this rule: "The one who is unwilling to work shall not eat," (II Thess. 3:10, NIV). Some of the Bible verses that discouraging depending on others "So that you may walk properly before outsiders and be dependent on one," (I Thess. 4:12, ESV); "Then the Lord said, "It is not good that the man should be alone; I will make him a helper fit for him," (Gen. 2:18, ESV).

Obsessive Compulsive Disorder

OCD stands for Obsessive Compulsive Disorder. This is basically, "A disorder in which people have recurring, unwanted thoughts, ideas or sensations (obsessions) that make them feel driven to do something (compulsion), The repetitive behaviors, such as hand washing, checking on things or cleaning, can significantly interfere with a person's daily activities and social interactions."[93] (American Psychiatric, www.psychiatry.org,

---

[92] (https://docs.google.com/document/d/1ORRkug4KmbcJq6wsiMkuZoe2wJGLNy4 ESvnVjjfXsJc/edit, Accessed February 2, 2021).

[93] (American Psychiatric, www.psychiatry.org, and https://www.psychiatry.org/patients-families/ocd/what-is-obsessive-compulsive-disorderAccessed February 2, 2021).

and https://www.psychiatry.org/patients-families/ocd/what-is-obsessive-compulsive-disorderAccessed February 2, 2021). People with OCD suffer from stressful thoughts and repetitive behaviors. They are addictive to such behaviors of which if they do those behaviors, can cause great stress. The OCD becomes a second to some people and becomes part of life. "Obsessions are recurrent and persistent thoughts, impulses, or images that cause distressing emotions such as anxiety or disgust. Many people with OCD recognize that the thoughts, impulses, or images are a product of their mind and are excessive or unreasonable... Compulsions are repetitive behaviors or mental acts that a person feels driven to perform in response to an obsession. The behaviors typically prevent or reduce a person's distress related to an obsession,"[94] Those who have OCD should be aware not to normalize their abnormality and think they are normal. They should try to avoid those behaviors to gravitate them and bit by bit eliminate the behaviors.

The Bible has many verses that God instructs us to desist from bad behaviors and to be self-controlled, "For God gave us a spirit not of fear but of power and love and self-control," (II Tim 1:7, ESV); "Casting all your anxiety on him, because he cares for you," (I Peter 5:7, ESV); "Therefore do not be anxious about tomorrow, for tomorrow will be anxious for itself. Sufficient for the day is its own trouble," (Matt. 6:34, ESV); "In peace I will both lie down and sleep; for you alone, O LORD, make me dwell in safety," (Psalm 4:8, ESV); "Fear not, for I am with you; be not dismayed, for I am your God; I will help you, I will uphold you with my righteous hand," (Isaiah 41:10, ESV); "Whoever trusts in his own mind is a fool, but he who walks in wisdom will be delivered," (Proverbs 28:26, ESV), "Cast your burden on the LORD, and he will sustain you' he will never permit righteous to be moved," (Psalm 55:22, ESV), "When the cares of my heart are many, your consolations clever my soul," (Psalm 94:19, ESV), "Then the Lord knows how to rescue the godly from trials, and to keep the unrighteous under punishment until the day of judgement," (II Peter 2:9, ESV), "Anxiety in a man's heart weighs him down, but a good makes him glad," (Proverbs 12:25, ESV); "For God gave us a spirit not of fear but of power and love and self-control," (II Tim 1:7, ESV).

---

[94] Ibid.

Anxiety

Anxiety is being anxious of certain things or the uncertainty of things. Anxiety is "A mental health disorder characterized by feelings of worry, anxiety, or fear that are strong enough to interfere with one's daily activities… Examples of anxiety disorders include panic attacks, obsessive compulsive disorder, and post traumatic disorder," "Anxiety is a normal and often healthy emotion. However, when a person regularly feels disproportionate levels of anxiety, it might become a medical disorder. Anxiety disorders form a category of mental health diagnoses that lead to excessive nervousness, fear, apprehension, and worry,"[95] (Medical News Today, https://www.medicalnewstoday.com, Accessed February 2, 2021). The anxiety disorder includes social phobia, agoraphobia, phobias, and many disorders associated with the anxiety.

The Bible has a lot of Scriptures that counsel those who have anxiety disorder. God counsels through His Word, "When anxiety was great within me, your consolation brought me joy," (Psalm 94:19, NIV); "Do not let your hearts be troubled. Believe in God and believe in me," (John 14:1, NIV); "For I am convinced that neither death nor life, neither angels nor demons, neither present nor the future, nor any powers, neither height nor depth, nor anything else in all creation, will be able to separate us from the love of God that is in Christ Jesus our Lord," (Romans 8:38-39, NIV); "I sought the LORD, and He delivered answered me from all my fears," (Psalm 34:4, NIV); "I want you to be free from anxieties," (I Cor. 7:32, ESV); "Say to those who have an anxious heart, 'Be strong; fear not! Behold, your God will come with vengeance, with the recompense of God. He will come and save you," (Isaiah 35:4, ESV); "When I am afraid, I put my trust in you," (Psalm 56:3, ESV); "And which of you by being anxious can add a single hour to his span of life?" (Matt. 6:27, ESV); "Casting all your anxieties on him, because he cares for you," (I Peter 5:7, ESV); "Now may the Lord of peace himself give you peace at all times in every way. The Lord be with you," (II Thess. 3:16, ESV); "Do not be anxious about anything, but in everything by prayer and supplication with thanksgiving let your requests be made known to God," (Phil. 4:6, NIV); "Therefore

---

[95] (Medical News Today, https://www.medicalnewstoday.com, Accessed February 2, 2021).

do not be anxious about tomorrow, for tomorrow will be anxious for itself. Sufficient for the day is its own trouble," (Matt. 6:34, ESV); "Anxiety in a man's heart weights him down, but a good word makes him glad, (Proverbs 12:25, ESV); "When the righteous cry for help, the LORD hears and delivers them out of all their troubles," (Psalm 34:17, ESV).

Addiction

Addiction is a condition one is being added to such as substance, a thing or activity and has become a psychological and physical habit that one is failing to stop which may result in harming the individual. According to American Society of Addiction Medicine, it is defined as, "Addiction is a complex, chronic brain condition influenced by genes and the environment that is characterized by substance use or compulsive actions that continue despite harmful consequences... The behavior causes problems for the individual or those around them. So instead of helping the person cope with situations or overcome problems, it tends to undermine these abilities."[96]

Scott and Lambert assert, "Then, in a counseling session in February (we had begun counseling in October), Julie admitted that she had begun drinking daily-resuming patterns of alcohol addiction that had been dormant for several years. She had grown up in a troubled home with two alcoholic parents and developed serious problems herself. Her drunkenness was doubly damaging-the problem of the alcohol itself was compounded by her mixing it with prescriptions."[97] Addiction becomes something one depends on to survive.

Depression: Use of hypnosis in therapy

Depression is one the most experienced phenomenon on both children and parents. In the secular, clinical psychology has its own way of therapy that is in line with their standards and protocol. Their therapy is scientific oriented with the out that have facts and evidence that can be proven. However, even within the field of clinical psychology, there is a deeply

---

[96] American Society of Addiction Medicine. <u>Definition of Addiction</u>. Published September 15, 2019.

[97] Stuart Scott and Heath Lambert, *Counseling the Hard Cases*, (Nashville: B & H Publishers), 2012, p. 266.

divided scholarly debate culminating from the evidenced-based treatment of depression using depressants in therapy or interpersonal psychotherapy. "In the United States, psychopharmacological approaches and certain forms of psychotherapy, particularly cognitive behavior therapy (CBT) and interpersonal psychotherapy (IPT) are generally recommended as treatments of choice for depression,"[98] McCann B., and Landers S., (2010), Hypnosis in the Treatment of Depression: Considerations in Research Designs and Methods, HHS Public Access, Apr. (2), 147-164. The hypothesis alludes that the empirically, validated treatment using antidepressant can also treat major psychiatric disorders. "Types of research support deemed appropriate for determining whether a particular form of psychotherapy has solid footing as evidence-based have been delineated by a task force of the American Psychological Association (APA). Despite the conclusion that cognitive Behavioral Therapy (CBT) from meta-analysis indicated that it was superior treatment for depression, the research indicates that they are no particular forms of therapy that is above or superior than the other therapies but that they are all equally important in their own context for different patients. "In fact, there was a slight advantage for interpersonal psychotherapy, and nondirective supportive psychotherapy was somewhat less efficacious,"[99] McCann and Landers (2010).

In the context of hypnosis treatment of depression, Yapko proposes that, "hypnosis has relevance to the treatment of depression because hypnosis can help build positive expectancy regarding treatment, address numerous depressive symptoms (including insomnia and rumination), and modify patterns of self-organization (such as cognitive, response, attentional, and perceptual styles) that contribute to depressed thinking and mood"[100] Michael Yapko (editor), in McCann and Lander (2010). They are some other approaches to use hypnosis to treat depression such as retrieval of past positive experience, the development of copying skills, augmenting interpersonal psychotherapy, and enhancing cognitive behavior therapy, McCann and Landers, (2010), https://www.ncbi.nlm.

---

[98] McCann and Landers, (20100), https://www.ncbi.nlm.nih.gov/pmc/articles/PMC2856099/#R48.

[99] Ibid.

[100] Ibid.

nih.gov/pmc/articles/PMC2856099/#R48. The clinicians are reluctant to use hypnosis to treat patients because the research concluded that hypnosis treatment of depression is harmful to some individuals. "We now turn to a description of several research methodologies and their suitability for exploring the treatment of depression using hypnotic methods. The first of these, the randomized controlled trial (RCT), is the current "gold standard" for empirically supported treatments (ESTs) and is a resource-intense methodology generally best suited to research settings. Two additional methods, single-case design and benchmarking are methods that can be more readily implemented within a clinical practice setting and may address some of the shortcomings of RCT approaches,"[101] McCann and Lander, (2010). The research reveals that the hypnosis does not authenticate the hypnosis as a treatment of depression to certain individuals because of its nature and whether hypnosis is a useful therapeutic strategy in treating depression.

Interpersonal Psychotherapy

Interpersonal psychotherapy approach has proven to be effective to practice if the skills, techniques, and interventions are utilized and the practice. "In highlighting both the covert and overt levels of these relational phenomena and their reciprocity, the interpersonal approach also provides a framework for seamlessly integrating concepts and techniques associated with other treatment approaches to PDS"[102] (Anchin, 1982a, 1982b, 2002; Pincus & Cain, 2008, 113). Interpersonal therapy focuses on specific problems of the client and can reduce the symptoms and can create good relationships. It can enhance problem solving and increase communication skills needed to anchor relationships. "These promote interpersonal awareness and learning, resulting in improved relational capacity and symptom reduction.

---

[101] Ibid. McCann and Lander, (2010).

[102] Anchin, J. C., & Pincus, A. L. (2010). *Evidence-based interpersonal psychotherapy with personality disorders*: Theory, components, and strategies. In J. J. Magnavita (Ed.), *Evidence-based treatment of personality dysfunction: Principles, methods, and processes* (pp. 113–166).

The social learning processes promote both intrapersonal and interpersonal change and enhance communication skill,"[103] (Anchin, 1982. p. 117).

Interpersonal Psychology approach to practice presents both benefits as well challenges. The benefits for using interpersonal psychology approach are that it helps to identify problems expressed in emotions, learning skills to foster good rapport, and it focuses on specific problem areas that need to be addressed. It can assist to solve problems, conflicts, disputes thus, improves the therapist's skills of communication by addressing issues such as depression, anxiety, and be able to administer treatment and symptoms for social adjustment for clients. The other benefits for interpersonal psychotherapy approach are that it strengthens relationships that can serve as support network for the benefit of the therapist. "Across all therapeutic modalities, nothing predicts good out come as reliably as the patient's experience of the therapist as warm, caring, and genuine, and, thus, the patient's experience of being seen, understood and helped,"[104] (Safran, J. D., & Muran, J. C. 2000), Accessed January 10, 2021. Interpersonal Psychotherapy approach creates a symbiotic relationship with the client if it is done with empathy and professionalism. It is a type of therapy structured model for treating mental health issues which is timely in the process it improves the interpersonal relationships. It is a brief or a short-structured therapy that produces immediate results.

Interpersonal psychotherapy comes with some challenges and limitations that the therapist should be aware of. When you are with the client in the process of therapy, the therapist has to empathize with the client but sometimes the clients do not recognize one's empathy. Instead, they would attack you verbally. "The therapist should be caring, non-judgmental, inspire hope, be able to repair ruptures and to find new ways that are better for the clients but sometimes the clients do not see the way out,"[105] (American Psychological Association, Producer,2009), Accessed January 15, 2021. The challenges and limitations for therapists is to guide the clients; it sometimes becomes surmountable. It can also enhance active

---

[103] Ibid. Anchin, 1982. p. 117.

[104] Safran, J. D., & Muran, J. C. (2000). *Negotiating the therapeutic alliance: A relational treatment guide.* New York, NY: Guilford Press. Accessed January 9, 2020, from Walden Library Database.

[105] (American Psychological Association, Producer,2009), Accessed January 15, 2021

and non-judgmental treatment that address depression, grief and anxiety disorder, bipolar and social phobia.

The cultures of the clients play importable roles in determining the types of therapy to administer. "The challenges of the therapists with regards to cultures of their clients is to understand the cultures fully. Their belief systems, cultures, traditions, norms, ethics, religions, and family can be a big challenge to the therapists. Therefore, to contextualize the clients' cultures may be a challenging experience,"[106] (APA, 2009), Accessed January 16, 2021. Gender issues can be a challenge for the therapists. Some clients lean to certain sexual orientations and it becomes very hard to discuss gender disparities when they don't believe in certain sextual orientations of other people that they love. Even if the therapist does not believe in certain sexual orientations, he/she should go beyond his/her belief systems. The therapist should create security for the clients, and sometimes it is challenging to convince the clients. In the same vein, the client in IPT must be willing to make some changes in their life for the therapy to be effective because the therapeutic process is considered to be client motivated and driven. It is client centered and with disparity of populations and cultural differences, to some cultures the IPT works perfect but to some cultures it does not.

When it comes to Biblical Counseling, which is Christ-Centered, Bible-Based and Holy Spirit-Empowered is breaking point and point of departure with Clinic Psychology. When each member of the family is affected and traumatized emotionally, spiritually, and physically, depression kicks in. If the family is affected by the disease or any issue that traumatize them, the church is also affected. Sheri Johnson and Adele Hayes write,

> Because of its prevalence, depression has been described as the common cold of mental illness. To receive a diagnosis of major depression, an individual must experience the following symptoms for a period of 2 weeks or more: sad mood or loss of pleasure, with at least four other symptoms such as sleep disturbance, appetite or weight

---

[106] Ibid. (American Psychological Association, Producer,2009), Accessed January, 16, 2021.

changes, psychomotor agitation, or retardation, fatigue, feelings of worthlessness or guilt, diminished ability to think or concentrate, and recurrent thoughts of death or suicide.[107]

To deal with depression, a counselor should know a number of factors, including an assessment of the period of the disease a pending issue one has discovered he/she has, family relationships, the individual's financial resources and assets, faith and belief in God, and how one views his/her sickness.

Depression as a Social Issue

The origin of depression varies from individual to individual and society to society. In reference to social issues affecting the children, or when someone has been diagnosed with the disease, they encounter a number of challenges which acerbate depression. The children or parent think deeply as to how they are in such a situation, why it happened to them, and they want to find a solution for it. When they spend much time thinking about how and why they are entangled in the web of suffering, they fall into depression. Janice Wood Wetzel explains,

> Our knowledge of depression dates back to 1033 B.C. in the Old Testament where King Saul in the book of 1 Samuel 16:14-23 recounts recurrent symptoms depression and suicide. . . For the first time, the mental disorders were attributed to brain pathology which in turn was said to affect thought and action.[108]

For example, cancer victims suffer from depression because they are sad that sooner or later they will die. They ponder death, day and night, reflecting on their past experiences with regret and thinking of the future without their children, spouses, and family members.

These thoughts flash through their minds all the time and affect

---

[107] Sheri L. Johnson and Adele M. Hayes, *Stress, Coping and Depression* (Mahwah, NJ: Lawrence Erlbaum Associates, 2000), ix.

[108] Janice Wood Wetzel, *Clinical Handbook of Depression* (New York: Gardner, 1984), 1.

their emotions, thus creating depression. Some can conceal depression consciously while others hide behind a mask of denial. Wetzel continues,

> In all cases, gentle probing will reveal a dysphonic mood state, replete with anxiety, guilt, and resentment. . . Difficulty with thinking processes is characteristic of almost all depressed people. Problems with concentration and decision making are a direct result. Negative rumination about the world, the self, and the future has been casually linked to depression as well, often encouraged recurrent suicidal thoughts.[109]

Social withdrawal is a common behavior associated with depressed people who might have lost interest in social activity and relationships of all kinds. For some, their motor responses are grossly affected while others are easily agitated, hostile, or irritated. As a result, physical function is also affected. Wetzel outlines diagnostic signs and symptoms of depression:

> Affective feeling state of sadness, dejected, fearfulness, anxiety, inadequacy, anger, guilt, confusion, tiredness, hopelessness, irritability. Cognitive thoughts process; negative view of the world, irrational beliefs, recurrent thoughts of death, self-reproach, low self-esteem, denial, slow thinking, disinterest in activities (people, pleasure), confused thoughts, poor concentration, agitation. Behavioral activity; dependence, submissiveness, poor communication skills, controlled by others, crying, withdrawal, inactivity, careless appearance, slowed motor responses. Physical functioning; low energy, weakness, fatigue sleep disturbance, weight loss, fatigue, appetite disturbance, indigestion, constipation diarrhea, nausea, muscle aches and headaches, tension, sex-drive disturbance.[110]

---

[109] Ibid. Wetzel, Clinical Handbook of Depression, 7.
[110] Ibid. 9

The Symptoms of Depression

Depression symptoms are synonymous with cancer. The pastor or counselor must be able to know the symptoms in order to counsel with informed observation and knowledge of what he/she is dealing with. As much as the member of the family/church may not disclose his/her disease, the counselor must be able to probe with wisdom.

The Effects of Depression

Depression affects the mind, emotions, and soul. The psyche of a human being can be affected by circumstances and situations, hence stress and depression are the result of such psychological disorder.

Nerve cells communicate to each other through electrical signals and brain chemicals. The following diagrams show the normal nerve cell communication in the brain. The brain functions normal. R. Ingalla and N. Oliver explain,

> This brain chemical then docks onto receptors of a second nerve cell. If enough chemical attaches on to the receptors, the second nerve cell is activated if it wasn't removed, the chemical would keep docking onto the receptors and nerve communication would be a constant nonsensical 'chatter' if a nerve cell is unhealthy (i.e., not working well), it generally has less receptors on its surface this makes it difficult for chemicals to attach and activate the nerve cell and keep the chain reaction going. A nerve cell that isn't activated on a regular basis becomes more and more unhealthy and can eventually delete unhealthy nerve cells in the brain are unlikely to have a major impact on overall brain function, but if many nerve cells in one brain area aren't working properly, effects can become very bad this is what happens in depression; the nerve

cells in certain areas of the brain are unhealthy and not working properly.[111]

Figure 2 illustrates how depression occurs on the individual who has become chemically unbalanced. Figure 1 illustrates normal nerve cells 1 to nerve cell 2.

Counseling the individual can be therapeutic, but if the depression is beyond reach, it may require medication. Figures 2 shows the process and impact if depression has not been addressed. It is important to understand the process and what the member of the church goes through when being counseled, because depression is the number one culprit in shortening the life of cancer patients and a cause of death. The skills of the counselor need to be of that of a professional counselor in order to get the best result for the counselee and the family members who anticipate full recovery and a better future. In the figure, the brain should receive enough oxygen and fuel needed for the brain to function well. R. Ingall and N. Oliver explain, "Diagram 2 shows the attempted activation of an unhealthy nerve cell without anti-depressant medication; diagram 3 shows the same, but with anti-depressant medication."[112] The attempted activation with antidepressant medication does not necessarily bring normality or stability. Through biblical counseling, the patient can come in grips with reality and recover from depression as the counselor helps the counselee to heal.

Redirecting the Counselee to Christ: Counseling Depression

In biblical counseling, the Scriptures point those who are depressed to Christ. "The thief on the cross looked to Jesus and asked, 'Jesus, remember me when you come into your kingdom.' Jesus answered, him, "Today you be with me in paradise" (Luke 23:42-43 NIV). When someone has lost hope in life, the counselor must refer or redirect the counselee to Christ because he is the bread of life, and the living water: "I am a good shepherd;

---

[111] R. Ingalla and N. Oliver, "Depression Beater/ Understanding Depression," 12, accessed January 8, 2021, http://www.depressionbeater.com/Understanding-Depression,(2270954).htm.

[112] R. Ingall and N. Oliver, "Depression—A Misunderstood Illness: Understanding and Treating Depression," accessed January 9, 2021, www.Depression- a Misunderstood Illness: Understanding and Treating Depression.

I know my sheep and my sheep know me," (John 10:14-15 NIV). Christ is the resurrection and life. "I am the resurrection and the life. The one who believes in me will live, even though they die" (John 11:25 NIV).

How does one counsel those who are depressed because of cancer? The first tool to be used is the Bible, the Word of God. Teaching members to cast their burdens on Christ is the first instruction to be shared with the depressed (Matt 11:28 NKJV). Job's three friends gave him bad counsel, accusing him of sinning against God (Job 2:11-13 NKJV). The first friend, Eliphaz, accused Job of sinning against God and of folly and said that therefore he was chastised by God; Job refuted the notion. The second friend, Bildad, accused Job of sinning and told him that he needed to repent because the wicked are punished; Job refused to listen to the accusation and pleaded with God instead. The third friend, Zophar, also urged Job to repent of his sins against God because he was wicked; Job answered his critics and maintained his integrity. His wife also asked him to curse God and die but Job refused and did not sin against God. Job demonstrates the love of God, perseverance, endurance, faith in God, and trusting the Lord in every circumstance. The counselor can refer the counselee to Job's experience as an example of not giving up faith in God.

In order to assist people with cancer or any life issues, certain counseling skills are required. Demitri Papolos and Janice Papolos state,

> In the most fundamental sense of the word, psychotherapy is a dialogue between two people where the patient has the respectful attention of a professional trained to elicit information. The professional, through clarification and interpretation, helps the person see things about him or herself in a realistic light-one not by a lingering sense of worthlessness or victimization. . . Psychotherapy can strengthen the capacity to cope, help the person to understand and come to terms with the vulnerability, and develop an adaptive way of coping with interpersonal

problems that emerge or are magnified as a result of the illness.[113]

In Biblical Counseling, the approach is Bible-oriented. Family members can support the patient if they are given information, for family involvement makes a critical difference in the life of a cancer person.

In counseling cancer, it is imperative to actively involve family members. The counselor guides and encourages the sick person to cope with the disease and to deal with anxiety, emotions, and frustration. Papolos and Papolos write,

> There are stages of recognition, adjustment, and adaptation to illness and each family travels through the stages in its own time and in its own fashion. Many factors influence the family's initial response to the onset of the illness: some members need to protect with the cloak of denial; almost all invent theories or take responsibility in an attempt to explain the changes in behavior. Each family is actually a caretaking system that over time has established rules, expectations, and basic assumption about caring for each other.[114]

There is a cultural tendency, to attempt to shield children from the unpleasant realities of life and of the illness at home. However, children are very sensitive and can imagine fast and terrible things about what would happen if their father or mother dies. Children become confused and anxious about their future. If their emotions explode, they are filled with fear, anxiety, uncertainty, and confusion.

There is a need for gradual explanation from one parent about the challenges and the predicament they would face. Children who participate and are involved in their parents' health challenges, happiness, and sorrows usually develop strength and a sense of belonging and worthiness when

---

[113] Demitri F. Papolos and Janice Papolos, *Overcoming Depression* (New York: Harper Perennial, 1992), 177.
[114] Ibid. 249

confronted with death. They are more able to cope with the death of loved ones than those who are left in the dark.

The church becomes the larger family to console, comfort, guide, counsel, pray for, encourage, empower, and support family members. The children, orphans, widows, and widowers should find refuge in the church. The pastor or counselor should prepare those who are dying to put their hope in Christ as they share the everlasting love and grace of Christ Jesus.

Suicidal Thoughts

Human behavior is very complex and hard to understand. King Solomon wrote about the vanity of life: "The words of the Preacher, the son of David, King in Jerusalem. Vanity of vanities, saith the Preacher, vanity of vanities; all is vanity" (Eccl 1:1-2 KJV). Life becomes vanity, i.e., meaningless, when hope is gone.

Life becomes meaningless as people face an unpredictable future with misery. The person is filled with anxiety, fear, confusion, stress, and depression, and sometimes finds it difficult to cope with life and sometimes resort to end his/her life immediately. Suicide is one of the ways and means people with stress or mental illness to end their lives. There are many ways people commit suicide because of circumstances or situations. To understand suicide, one must understand human behavior. Douglas Jacobs and Herbert N. Brown point out that there are basically four kinds of suicides:

> Altruistic suicides are literally required by society. Here, the customs or rules of the group 'demand' suicide under certain circumstances. "Egoistic" suicide occurs when the individual has too few ties with his community. Demands to live do not reach him. "Anomic" suicides are those that occur when the accustomed relationship between an individual and his society is suddenly shattered, such as the shocking, immediate loss of a loved one, a close friend, a job, or even a fortune. "Fatalistic" suicides derive from

excessive regulation. Examples would be persons such as slaves or prisoners whose futures are piteously blocked.[115]

The biblical counselor must know the types of suicide that people resort to as options to end their lives. The basic understanding of suicide in the context of these four categories shows that human behavior has great influence from social, psychological, biological, and spiritual phenomena. A counselor needs to understand what may cause the client or church member to commit suicide.

Voluntary and Involuntary Suicides

Suicides are planned, calculated, and thought-out behaviors, not impulsive.

Suicide relates to schizophrenia, alcoholism, addiction and also paresis. "In constructing the events preceding a death by means of a 'psychological autopsy' it was concluded that suicidal behavior is often a form of communication, a cry for help' born out of pain and anguish and a plea for response."[116] At times, suicidal thoughts come to individuals without planning, but through mental sickness. There are involuntary suicide and voluntary suicide. Those who involuntarily commit suicide may do so without having an intention to kill themselves but only do so because they have been pushed to reach the highest level of social or economic reasons. In other situations, someone may love another so much that if he/she is heart-broken, he/she may commit suicide. Some may commit suicide because they want to die to appease their gods.

Everstine writes, "Then there are the most tragic of those who must end their lives—the dying. They include people who have only just been told that they are being consumed by disease or old age."[117]

Those who are finding life become difficult and are hopeless and believe that them lives have come to an end and commit suicide before they get sicker. Prisoners who have been either sentenced to death or life imprisonment are also likely to commit suicide.

---

[115] Douglas Jacobs and Herbert N. Brown, *Suicide: Understanding and Responding* (Madison, CT: International University Press, 1989), 6

[116] Ibid. 13.

[117] Louis Everstine, *The Anatomy of Suicide: Silence of the Heart* (Springfield, WA: Charles C. Thomas, 1998), 20.

Everstine states,

> The compulsion to do the deed carries such urgency that it creates its own reality, and within that context it can truly be considered "involuntary." The best example is that of the grand master of human motivation, Sigmund Freud himself. His recently released last diary tells how he dealt with death when, at the age of 83, he felt that it was taking too long to arrive. Finally exhausted by pain from cancer of the jaw that he had resisted so many years, he asked his doctor to give him just enough extra morphine that would end the ordeal.[118]

Sigmund Freud argued throughout his lifetime and believed that the truth about one's self would set them free, however, he finally requested to be given extra morphine so that he could die. King Saul voluntarily commanded his armor-bearer to end his life:

> The fighting grew fierce around Saul, and when the archers overtook him, they wounded him critically. Saul said to his armor-bearer, "Draw your sword and run me through, or these uncircumcised fellows will come and run me through and abuse me." (1 Sam 31:3-4 NIV)

Involuntary suicide occurs when the person does not have control of him/herself because of pain and the physician terminates his/her life with the consent of the relatives.

Voluntary suicide is when a person decides to terminate his/her life by choice.

> Suicide of the voluntary sort is the most negative of human actions because it mocks whatever means to be human. It is the most unnatural of actions because it defies the

---

[118] Ibid. 21.

survival instinct. . . It is the worst among absurd crimes because it contradicts itself.[119]

Prevention and Reversing Suicidal Thoughts

Counseling children or parents with suicidal thoughts is a challenging task, but it must be done quickly before the person kills him/herself. First, the counselor or pastor must discern or detect the motives. Everstine writes,

> Detecting it, uncovering its causes, and acting swiftly to intervene are the skills that most clinicians possess intuitively. . . Diverting suicidal ideation with other reframing therapy that seeks to achieve and rest on three guiding principles: diagnosis, diagnosis, diagnosis.[120]

Diagnosis is important because many people who commit suicide do not come for help and do not inform their counselors that they want to kill themselves. Their thoughts are usually hidden and cannot be detected easily.

Two theories can be compared in the process of committing suicide: Stekel's theory and Freud's theory. These theories are similar but they differ with one stage. Stekel argues that the person who wants to commit suicide becomes deficient in relating to other people and thinks others should die but he/she is not able to express his/her wish in action. He asserts that anyone who wants to kill him/herself, first he/she would have thought of killing someone else and wishes someone was killed. Figure 5 illustrates the repressed superego, which leads to repressed murderous impulses that start with repressed impulse, then the feeling of guilt, and self- destruction. The guilty conscience (superego) drives someone to kill. His/her view is that if one wishes to kill someone else and fails to take the action, he/she can then commit suicide Freud borrowed the thought from Stekel:[121]

---

[119] Ibid. 23.

[120] Everstine, *The Anatomy of Suicide*, 30

[121] Everstine, *The Anatomy of Suicide*, 31.

> In this equation, Freud has inserted a "melancholic state" between the guilt feelings, as identified by Stekel, and the suicidal act. This state, melancholia, is the same as the one we call "depression." It is one of the most common forms of mental illness, and its role in the meaning of suicide.[122]

Stekel and Freud's secular theories can help to understand the emotional levels of the patient who wants to commit suicide, however, a biblical counselor uses the Bible as the main source to counsel a patient. A counselor needs to be able to detect and prevent suicides. A suicidal person is seeking to escape pain and wants to draw people's attention to show them that he/she has had a problem that was too difficult to solve.

> Alec Roy explains, Suicide is best understood not so much as an unreasonable act-every suicide seems logical to the person who commits it given that person's major premises, styles of syllogizing, and constricted focus-as it is a reaction to frustrated psychological needs. A suicide is committed because of thwarted or unfulfilled needs.[123]

The common emotion in suicide is compounded by hopelessness and helplessness. If family members, the church, the community, and friends neglect the needs of people with mental illness, some resort to killing themselves to escape stigmatization, abandonment, deteriorated illness, shame, guilt, frustration, depression, and stress.

---

[122] Ibid. 31.
[123] Ibid. 32.

CHAPTER FOUR
CHOOSING A LIFE PARTNER

Seeking the Will of God

Choosing a life partner is one of the fundamental, choice that God gave to humankind. It should not be taken hastily but with deep prayer, planning, guidance, wisdom. Marriage was designed by God and it is approved of God, a man and a woman. "He who finds a wife finds a good thing and obtains favor from the Lord," (Proverbs 18:22, ESV). "For this reason, a man will leave his father and mother and be united to his wife, and the two will be one flesh," (Ephesians 5:31; Genesis 2:24, NKJV). God's original concept of instituting marriage was for both the male and female to unite and become one flesh. The relationship is permanent and a vow that bond the two forever. Man's parents are not to interfere with the new family that has been created. For the relationship to be ideal and cemented, the husband and wife become one flesh.

CHOOSING A LIFE PARTNER

1. WHEN is the Appropriate Age for Marriage?

"[124]The average ideal for marriage is 25 for Women and 27 for Men, (New Jersey Gallup's Annual Polls on Values and beliefs in America," https://

---

[124] (New Jersey Gallup's Annual Polls on Values and beliefs in America," https://news.gallup.com/poll/23404/ideal-age-marriage-women-men.aspx), Accessed, March 1, 2021.

news.gallup.com/poll/23404/ideal-age-marriage-women-men.aspx),
Accessed, March 1, 2021. There is a standard and appropriate age for
marriage according to the laws of every country and culture in the world.
What is the Biblical standard? Mary the mother of Jesus was between 12-
14 years old when she was betrothed to Joseph, according to Jewish ancient
custom. It is thought that Mary was 16 years old when Jesus was born and
Joseph around 18 years old (Matt. 1:18, NKJV). Isaac was 40 years old
when he married Rebecca (Gen. 25:20, NKJV).

2. WHERE do you Marry

The church is where you belong and date a born-again Christian. You
can date from your tribe, race or from your people. If you speak the same
language the better. Isaac married Rebecca, what a fascinating story of
love connection, (Genesis 24, NKJV). However, one may choose a life
partner from another race or tribe but one must be prepared to align with
the expectations of the race or tribe and be able to balance your own race
or tribe with your partner's culture.

"Don't be unequally yoked with unbelievers. For what fellowship
has righteousness with lawless? And what communion has darkness with
darkness…" (2 Cor.6:14-16, NKJV). When oxen are unequally yoked,
they cannot perform the task set before them. Don't team up with
unbelievers. How can darkness be partnered with light? What fellowship
do righteousness and iniquity have in common.

3. WHY is Marriage Important?

a. "And the Lord God said, 'It is not good that a man should be
    alone; I will make him a helper comparable to fit him," (Gen.
    2:18-25, NKJV).
b. "To the unmarried and the widows, I say it is good for them to
    remain single, as I am. But if they cannot exercise self-control, they
    should marry. For it better to marry than to burn with passion"
    (I Cor. 7:8-9, ESV).

4. WHO to Marry?

It is a choice of every individual to choose their life partners according
to the qualities they desire. However, there are some cultures, traditions

and religions that can make some arrangements for marriages between families and that is acceptable to their own societies and communities' laws for marriage. The international legal age of marriage, especially, to 168 countries, is 18 years for girls. Other countries have exceptional customary laws who can marry younger than 18 with parental consents, boys included as well.

5. HOW do you Choose?

By listing what you want. Write a checklist and present to the Lord and believe that he will direct you always. "Commit your work to the Lord, and your plans will be established," (Proverbs 16:3, 9, NIV).

10 Qualities that One May Consider for a Life Partner

1. Choose someone whom you love and respect

To spend the rest of your life with some whom you love and respect is the most fulfilling purposes of life ever. When choosing a life partner be sure to choose someone who will love and respect you, your ambitions, your vision and your aspirations. Mutual respect is one of the defining traits to look for in a life partner.

2. Emotional Maturity

Choose a life partner who is emotionally mature and who will be able to control himself/herself with grace and always well balanced in everything. Choose a partner who is able to manage his/her anger and has ager manage skills. Anger issues may manifest in the future and you may not be able to deal with it if you discover his/her reactions to issues later in life.

3. Willingness to Sacrifice

Choose someone who is willing to play his/her part in making the relationship to work. Each partner must be willing to invest time, skills, wisdom, energy and everything to make the marriage work.

4. Honest life partner

Choose a life partner who is honest, dependable, trustworthy, truthful and faithful. To have someone in the house, a partner who cheats, who is not trustworthy, not truthful, one who lies and not faithful, can bring misery in one's life.

5. Prayerful Life Partner

Choose a partner who is in tune with God and who is a prayerful partner and who knows where to go when you face the challenges of life. Choose a life partner who knows the Lord and who will encourage you to study the Word diligently, madidate on it and apply it in their lives.

6. Ability to assimilate in your family

Choose a life partner who is willing to assimilate into your family and to love them too. Your family will always be with you and they care for you. They will be a powerful support system in everything you do. Choose a life partner who will respect the members of your family and your consanguinity and who is willing bring unity within the family than division.

7. Able to forgive and Reconcile

Choose a life partner who is able to argue but is able to forgive and reconcile, easily. Avoid someone who keeps grudges after making arguments over some issues and does not forgive and not willing to reconcile.

8. Sympathetic and Empathetic

Choose a life partner who can feel your pain and be able to be part of the solution. Choose a life partner who has compassion, loving, caring, kind, and has a good heart for people, not cruel. Empathy goes beyond sympathy. It is getting into the shoes of the other person and experience someone's pain and finds the remedy or help and be able willing to alleviate the pain of another person.

9. Communication

Choose a partner who is able to communicate and understand the other person's feelings. Communication is a two-way transmission of a clear message between two or more people. Communication is the fundamental skills in any given relationships. If there is a communication breakdown, the relationship will collapse easily.

10. Patience and Tolerant

Choose a partner who has patience and is tolerant. Patience is one of the most important qualities which is required in a relationship. Marriage is requiring patience and tolerance of one other. We all have flaws and we make mistakes but if you have a life partner who is patient and is able bear with you, it is a treasure in the house.

The list goes on but these are basic qualities one may look into when choosing a life partner. It is important to understand that no one is perfect and no one will be able to find someone who is perfect. These are ten guidelines that will assist you to find some like you or better than yourself to partner with in your longevity. Remember that a good wife/husband comes from the Lord. "House and wealth are inherited from fathers, but a prudent wife is from the Lord," (Proverbs 19:14, ESV).

Marital Sex and Intimacy (1 Corinthians 7:1-5; 1 Corinthians 6:18-19, NKJV)

Celibacy is acceptable however, if someone cannot control himself and there is so much immorality, each man should have his own wife, and each woman her own husband. The church in Corinth had some issues with marriage and celibacy and responded with the admonition and instruction about marriage and being single. If one chooses to be single and devote his oneself to the service of the Lord without distraction, it is good. Paul spells out the temptations of the single person which can lead to impurity and he refers to the price Christ Jesus paid on the cross and he says that in the same manner, he uses his body to glorify God of which his body belongs to Christ. However, if one cannot control himself, he should marry. He also specifically says, when a husband or a wife marry, their bodies belong to their spouses not their own. Paul emphasizes the importance of sexual intimacy with the spouses in marriage, always except in times of prayer and fasting. In the holy union, both the husband and wife must recognize and honor interdependence to each other. The Christian couple should not deprive each other because they are one flesh and avoid temptations, they should not deprive each other of sex. If they are praying and fasting, or if it is temporary, then they should resume immediately in sex consummation.

In the same vein, Paul warns the Corinthians to flee sexual immorality, in (I Cor. 6:18-19, NKJV). Here, Paul addresses the seriousness of sin if one commits with his own body. He discusses those who are not married or those who are married but engage in sexual immorality. In the first passages of (I Cor. 7:1-4, NKJV). Paul discusses those who are single and that they remain single and devote their lives to the service to the Lord. In the same passage, he discusses those who are married to seek to satisfy each other as husband and wife. In (I Cor. 6:18-19, NKJV), he emphatically warns those who engage in sexual immorality who are either single or married. He warns them to flee from sexual immorality and reminds them that their bodies are the temple of God who live in them and they should not abuse their bodies with filthy sexual conducts. He expounds that most sins have no direct effect on one's body, but sexual immorality directly affects one's body. Every believer is indwelt by the Holy Spirit. Therefore, it is an abomination to use the temple of God in which the Holy Spirit lives and use it for the evil purposes. Paul reminds the Corinthian church that we are not our own but we are possessed by the Holy Spirit.

Paul connects the two passages not on contradictory trajectory but in a complementary manner as both they point to spiritual and moral standard the believers should pursue as they no longer belong to the world and fulfilling the desires of flesh such as "For the sinful nature desires what is contrary to the spirit, and the spirit what is contrary to the sinful nature. They are in conflict with each other, so that you do not do what you want. But if you are led by the spirit, you are not under the law. The acts of the sinful nature are obvious: sexual immorality, impurity, and debauchery, idolatry and witchcraft, hatred, discord, jealousy, fits of rage, selfish ambition, dissensions, factions, and envy; drunkenness, orgies, and the like. I warn you, as I did before, that those who live like this will not inherit the kingdom of God." (Gal. 5:16-21, NLT).

Here, Paul warns the Galatians about their behaviors and conducts that are worldly. The same principles and standards are required to the Corinthian church. The fruit of the spirit the Corinthian church depicts are, "But the fruit of the spirit is love, joy, peace, patience, kindness, goodness, faithfulness, gentleness, and self-control. Against such things, there is no law," (Gal. 5:22-23, ESV).

Eight Types of Love

To put everything into the right perspectives, it is fundamental to discuss about what love is and the eight types of love that are presented by the ancient Greek. Mateo and Luna Sol, put it so beautifully that:

1. "Eros" or Erotic Love

- Named after Greek god of love and fertility
- Represents sexual passion and desire
- It is for procreation
- Can misused and abused which can lead to broken hearts
- It's powerful and can burn quickly
- Self-centered for physical pleasure
- Married couples can hit the bottom if they enter marriage without understanding.

2. "Philia" or Affectional Love

- Philia love is friendship love. The Ancient Greeks valued this type of love above "eros" as they considered a love between equals.
- Plato argued that physical attraction is not necessary part of love.
- Philia is love between friends who endure hard times together
- I can involve feelings of loyalty among friends, teammates to sacrifice for each other.

3. "Storge" or Familiar Love

- Can closely resemble "Philia" love in terms of love without physical attraction, "Storge" is kinship and consanguinity love of family.
- "Storge" is a natural form of affection between parents and their children, grand-children, cousins, uncles, aunts.
- "Storge" can found among childhood friends shared later as adults.
- Can become an obstacle when friends and family member don't align or do not support each other.

4. "Ludus" or Playful Love

- "Ludus" has erotic eros in it but it more than that. The Greeks considered Ludus as play form of love, for example, the affection between young lovers.
- Ludus is early stages of falling in love with someone e.g., the fluttering heart, flirting, teasing, and feelings of euphoria.
- Sometimes it can be long lasting in childhood relationships

5."Mania" or Obsessive Love

- "Mania" love is a type of love that leads a partner into a type of madness and obsessiveness.
- "Mania" love reinforces their own value as they suffer of poor self-esteem. The person wants love and be loved to find a sense of self-value.
- They can become so possessive and jealous lovers, desperately needing their partners to validate their worthiness.
- If the other partner fails to reciprocate, or indicates that the love affair is failing, can harm self, partner or commit suicide.

6. "Pragma" / Enduring Love

- "Pragma" or Enduring love has aged, matured and developed over time.
- It's beyond the physical, transcends the casual and formed over time.
- Married couples are the examples who have been together for a long time.
- It is not easily found. Some friends can develop into that.
- People spend life time trying to find this type of love but when they find it, fail to maintain it.
- "Pragma" is the result of effort on both sides. It's the love between the people who have learned to make compromises, have demonstrated patience and tolerance to make the relationship work.

7. "Philautia" or Self-Love

- The Greeks understood that for someone to care for others, first one must care for him/herself.
- "Philautia" is self-love in its healthiest form. Being comfortable in your skin, understanding yourself that you are created in the image of God (Psalm 139:14, NKJV), . After that one can then provide the love for others.
- You cannot share what you do not have. If you do not love yourself, you cannot love any else either.
- Find unconditional love for yourself, not pride but genuine love for your own.

8. "Agape" or Selfless Love

- "Agape" is the highest and most radical type of love, selfless and unconditional love.
- Not sentimental love but outpouring. Has nothing to do condition-based type of love.
- "Agape" love is spiritual love, unconditional, bigger that ourselves, boundless compassion, an infinity empathy.
- It is the purest form of love that is free from desires and expectations, and love regardless of the flaws and shortcomings of others.
- "Agape" love is the divine truth, the love that accepts, forgives and believes for our greater good.
- "Agape" love is sacrificial love that endures forever.[125]

Mateo and Luna Sol, (2012-2018), https://lonerwolf.com/contact, (Accessed February, 26, 2021).

---

[125] Mateo and Luna Sol, (2012-2018), https://lonerwolf.com/contact, (Accessed February 26, 2021).

CHAPTER FIVE
SEPARATION & DIVORCE

God's Word about Divorce

Divorce is not found in God's plan for marriage. However, Christ gave the reasons for divorce. To start with, we have to discuss the condition of man whether he can love his wife perfectly or whether the wife can submit to her husband perfectly and Paul stipulates in (Ephesians 5:22-33, NKJV). In fact, that's not possible because an unperfect perfect person cannot give any perfection to anyone. Total depravity of man means that man is not able to love God with all their hearts, mind, souls and strengths because of the fall. Human beings are egocentric, loving themselves not God by nature but reject His laws and rules. The original sin corrupted their nature and cannot please or obey God. "For all have sinned and come fall short of the glory of God," (Rom. 3:23, NIV). "As it is written: There is no one righteous, not even one," (Rom. 3:10, NIV). It is important to understand the doctrine of depravity in counseling because that's the premise to stand with to let everyone know that we have fallen and we cannot please God by nature. The counselors and the counselees must understand that they will continue making some mistakes because they are not one who is perfect. Therefore, counseling starts from the right standing before God and acknowledging that we need a Savior and the Holy Spirit to help us through this life. "If we say we have not sinned, we make him a liar and his word is not in us," (I John 1:10, ESV).

The man's nature is fallen and needs redemption. "And almost all things are by the law purged with blood; and without the shedding of blood, is no remission," (Hebrews 9:22, KJV). "All have sinned and come short of the glory of God," (Romans 3:23, NIV). Man needs to be redeemed and needs a Savior. Man's nature is corruptible and susceptible to sin every second and is dying every time. The psychological characteristics, the feelings and the behavior traits are evil to the core. "Now the works of the flesh are obvious: sexual immorality, moral impurity, promiscuity, idolatry, sorcery, hatred, strife, jealousy, outbursts of anger, selfish ambitions, dissensions, factions, envy, drunkenness, carousing, and anything similar," (Gal. 5:19-21, KJV).

The man's present condition is that he is a sinner and needs a Savior. Man is evil in his ways. "The Lord saw how great the wickedness of the human race had become on the earth, and that every inclination of the thoughts of the human heart was only evil all the time," (Genesis 6:5, NIV). However, if the man turns to God, repents and asks for forgiveness, God changes him to be a new creation and his condition is brought up to life just like Christ in His resurrection. "Therefore, if anyone is in Christ, the new creation has come: The old has gone behold he is a new creature: old things are passed away; behold, all things are become new," (II Cor.5:17, NIV).

God declared man and his wife shall be joined to be one. "For this reason, a man shall leave his father and his mother, and be joined to his wife; and they shall become one," (Gen: 2:24, NKJV). The divorce was not a plan of God but it is the sin that entered the world. Jesus declared, "It has been said, 'Anyone divorces his wife must give her a certificate of divorce. But I tell you that anyone who divorces his wife, except for sexual immorality, makes her the victim of adultery and anyone who married a divorced woman commits adultery," (Matt. 5:31-32, NIV). The basis of divorce is given by Jesus Christ himself in this text is the sexual immorality. If the wife is living in an abusive relationship, the churches may allow the wife to divorce her husband and vice versa. In the OT, divorce was permitted according to (Deut. 24:1-4, NIV). However, the punishment of adultery was not a divorce but stoning to death (Deut. 22:22, NIV). In the OT., divorce was permitted for other reasons rather than adultery because for adultery was not divorce but stoning the victim to death.

The issue of divorce and remarriage is complex, it has to be handled with prayer and seeking God's will. God's intention for marriage was for life only to be separated by death (Rom. 7:2, 3, NIV). God hates divorce (Mal. 2:16, NIV). God actually divorced Israel when they married other gods, the idols, allegorically, "I gave faithless Israel her certificate of divorce and sent her away because of all her adulteries... Because Israel's immorality mattered so little to her, she defiled the land and committed adultery with stone and wood. In spite of all this, her unfaithful sister Judah did not return to Me with all their heart, but only in pretense, (Jer. 3:8;10, NIV). Some Christian scholars think that (I Cor. 7:12-16, NIV) teaches that divorce can be acceptable when a believer is left by an unbeliever. Paul seems to allude that the believer is no longer under bondage in that case but that he/she is free to obtain divorce. The Church trends on the borderline when it comes to divorce and remarriage but the scripture is very clear about God's will. Love does not come from us but from God, (John 3:16, NIV).

The importance of James 4:1-5, NIV, is that it points to the source of strife, fights, quarrels, which is basically, selfishness, ego and the desire and pride of life. Sin that causes people to puff up and seek gratifications causes strife and fights among people. In previous texts, James had alluded that the wise man is a peace-loving man. He turns to confront the reasons they are unhappy and not peaceful homes. He then points out the reason there is strife, greed, anger, malice, envy, jealous, quarrels among Christian homes. The reason is simple, to satisfy lusts, pleasures, gain possessions, for selfish reasons. Christians fight in their homes and covet but we do not gain anything after all the fights. There is no peace in the Christian families because they focus on themselves not on God. God is the foundation of the family. Praying together and planning together can solve the problem of strife and quarreling. The family that prays together sticks together. Here James condemns love that is based on material things as idolatry. People value material things instead of seeking the will of God. James categorically, scorns those who love the world as they become the enemies of God. When they ask God, they don't get it because of the wrong motives and wrong priorities. Therefore, God does not answer their prayers because of wrong motives with wrong intentions. The world system consists of the lust of the eyes, the lust of flesh, and the pride of life that do not align with

God's will. Verse 5, is a breaking point. "Do you think that the Scripture says in vain, 'The Spirit who dwells in us yearns jealously?" (James 4:5, NKJV). The Spirit living in us does not envy or crave for the worldly things, the jealousy or lust of the world.

The couple has to be redirected and reminded of who they are in Christ and that the strife, quarrel, anger, bitterness, lust and love of self does not belong to God but it is the worldly standard. In God, there is no competition but it is a worldly spirit. In the context of (James 4:1-12, NKJV), especially from James 4:6, NKJV James turns to how God detests such behavior and attitude. God opposes the proud but shows favor to the humble. James points out that God wants humble people. Humility, submission to God's authority, compels God to give more grace to the humble. From James 4:6, NKJV, James gives hope and encouragement to those who adhere to God's plea to embrace His people. We are not to deal with natural desires alone but if we allow God to uproot and plant new spirit, all will work for the good to them that love God, to them who are called according to his purpose (Romans 8:28, NKJV). Here James quoted Proverbs 3:34, NKJV, God resists the proud. As such, couples in marriage should resist the devil and he will flee from them. James encourages the saint to draw near to God. God is the focus and the source of a happy family. Couples should confess to God and to each other with deep sorrow of sin, with lament and mourn and be humble before God. The couple would be referred to (Ephesians 5:22-33, NKJV) for counseling, what the wife is commanded to submit to her husband as she submits to Christ and the husband to love his wife as Christ loved the church. "Humble yourself before the Lord, and he will lift you up," (James 4:10, NIV).

James 4:11, 12, deals with censoriousness, speaking evil against a brother. The royal law demands us to love our neighbor not to speak evil against or to judge a brother, or neighbor or spouse for that matter. The spouses should love one another, encourage, sacrifice, cherish, protect each other and pray together to honor God in their marriage. The counsel to an abusive husband is what the Scripture says about the husband's wife and how she must be treated as a command. The person who abuses his wife has a spiritual problem, that is the first diagnosis. Apostle Paul in (Ephesians 5:25, NIV), instructs that, "Husbands, love your wives, just as Christ loved the church and gave himself for her., to make her holy, cleansing her with washing of water by the word." God gave husbands a command to love their wives as Christ loved the church and sacrificed for her. The husband who violets that command needs thorough counsel. Verbal abuse is the same as physical abuse if it is not worse with all depression, frustration and stress it brings with it. The wife has to be treated with respect and dignity, physically, spiritually and morally. Paul continues to say, "In the same way, husbands ought to love their wives as their own bodies. He who loves his wives loves himself. After all, no one ever hated his own body, but he feeds and cares for it, just as Christ does the church," (Eph. 5:25-29, NIV).

The husband needs to love his wife as himself, as one feeds, cares for himself, he should do so to his wife just like Christ does to the church. In the Old Testament, the commandment to love your wife is inferred. "The Old Testament does not contain an explicit "job description" for husbands. Nevertheless, it is possible to infer some of the major responsibilities of husbands toward their wives from various portions of the Hebrew Scriptures," Andreas and David continue to extract the facts about Old Testament excerpts about the mandate for the husbands to love their wives, "Among these are the following: (1) to love and cherish his wife and to treat with respect and dignity; (2) to bear primary responsibility for the marriage union ultimate over the family; (3) to provide food, clothing, and other necessitates for his wife." The Scriptures are very clear that any husband who abuses his wife stands condemned and repudiated by God and the Bibles. No one should ever do it because the two shall become one when united as a husband and wife. "For this reason, a man shall leave his father and mother and be united to his wife, and the two shall become one," (Eph. 5:31, NKJV).

God's Word about Reconciliation

The couple that is contemplating of divorce have a chance to talk over the controversial issues and the reasons for filing for divorce and can forgive, reconcile, and consider remarriage. The counselors, ministers and the courts usually give the couple a period of separation so that they think over the decision they want to take. Forgiveness in Greek is (*Aphine*), and it has a range of meanings which includes to remit a debt, to leave or abandon something done against you. Forgiveness is the turning away vengeance of a person who has wronged you. We have two types of forgiveness in the Bible. 1. God's justification and pardon for our sins of omission and commission. 2. Human forgiving and pardoning others and being forgiven by others of what one would have committed against them. Forgiveness by God stretching down to man's first sin, Adam and Eve who disobeyed God. When one realizes that he/she is sinner, turns around, repents and acknowledges Christ as the Lord of his/her life and believes in his/her heart, that Jesus died and rose again on the third day, will be saved (Rom. 10:10, NKJV). Therefore, God loved us so much that He provided the way to come back to Him and be reconciled to Him through His only Son, Jesus Christ (John 3:16, NKJV). Through Christ, we are forgiven and justified and sanctified because Jesus said, I am the Way, the Truth and the Life. No one comes to the Father except through me," (John 14:6, NKJV). Christ's sacrifice was necessary and required to satisfy God's justice. Jesus took the penalty on our behalf. Christ, therefore, instituted a new covenant with His blood. "This is my blood of the new covenant, which is poured out for many for the forgiveness of sin," (Matt. 26:28, NIV). Christ atoned for our sins. He was crucified but on the third day He rose from the dead, defeating death and its sting, (I Cor. 15:54-57, NIV).

"If we confess our sins, he is faithful and just to forgiveness us and cleanse us from all unrighteousness," (I John 1:8-9, NIV). God declares, "Then he adds: Their sins and lawless acts I will remember no more," (Hebrews 10:17, NIV). The Scriptures tell us that Christ is our redemption, "In him we have redemption through his blood, the forgiveness of sins, in accordance with the riches of God's grace," (Eph. 1:7, NIV). God overlooked ignorance in the past but He wants people to come to the Lord Jesus Christ. "In the past God overlooked such ignorance, but now he commands all people everywhere to repent," (Acts 17:30, NIV).

God has instructed us to forgive others because we have been forgiven. Christ gave us all the examples to forgive even our enemies. We have two kinds of relationships, the vertical, i.e., God with us and also the horizontal relationships, which are basically, between you and other fellows. God instructs us to forgive other people who wrong us. "For if you forgive other people when they sin against you, your heavenly Father will also forgive you. But if you do not forgive others their sins, your Father will not forgive your sins," (Matt. 6:14-15, NIV). To refuse to forgive others their sins is against God's command. "Bear with each other and forgive one another if any of you has a grievance against someone. Forgive as the Lord forgave you," (Col. 3:13, NIV). "Then Peter came to Jesus and asked, 'Lord, how many times shall forgive my brother or sister who sins against me?' Jesus answered, "I tell you the truth, not seven times, but seventy-seven times," (Matt. 18:21-22, NIV). God gives a chance to everyone to forgive. "For if you forgive other people when they sin against you, your heavenly Father will also forgive you," (Matt. 6:14, NIV). God instructs us not to judge other people, for the same judgement may befall on you. "Do not judge, and you will not be judged. Do not condemn, and will not be condemned. Forgive, and you will be forgiven," (Luke 6:37, NIV). It is imperative to confess your sins to God and also to one another, "Whoever conceals their sins does not prosper, but the one who confesses and renounces them finds mercy," (Proverbs 28:13, NIV).

God's Word about Remarriage

When the couple have ironed out their differences and discussed their controversial issues for pending divorce, they can turn to the Bible and find Scriptures that can revive and mend their broken relationships. The Scripture has been given to use to counsel, rebuke, correct, to encourage and of course, with great patience, to reconcile us to God and to each other, (II Tim. 4:2, NIV). The basis for remarriage is given in two folds in the Bible. The first reason to divorce is spelled out by the Scripture which addresses remarriage very clear. "I tell you that anyone who divorces his wife, except for sexual immorality, and marries another woman commits adultery," (Matt. 19:9, NIV). This is Christ's teachings to the church. "Anyone who divorces his wife and marries another woman commits adultery, and the man who married a divorced woman commits adultery," (Luke 16:18, NIV). The teaching is very clear in that if one divorces his wife or her husband, he/she should not remarry because if he/she does, he/she commits adultery, except in the case of being unfaithful of the other spouse. The second reason is alluded here, "But if the unbeliever leaves, let it be so. The brother or sister is not bound in such circumstances; God has called us to live in peace," (I Cor. 7:15, NIV).

Paul is emphatic in discussing and teaching. "To the married I give this command (not I, but the Lord): A wife must not separate from her husband. But if she does, she must remain unmarried or else be reconciled to her husband. And a husband must not divorce his wife," (I Cor. 7:10-11, NIV). The third reasons to remarry is when the spouse dies, then the remaining spouse is free to remarry if she wants. "For example, by law a married woman is bound to her husband as long as he is alive, but if her husband dies, she is released from the law that binds her to him. So then, if she has sexual relations with another man while her husband is still alive, she is called adulteress. But if her husband dies, she is released from that law and is not an adulteress if she marries another man." (Rom. 2-3, NIV). The ultimate mandate from the Lord is that He regards marriage high and the seriousness of marriage is echoed God Himself, "The man who hates and divorces his wife,' says the Lord, the God of Israel, 'does violence to the one he should protect,' says the Lord Almighty. So be on guard, do not be unfaithful." (Malachi 2:16, NIV). God respects and honors marriage and commands everyone to do the same, "Marriage should be honored by all, and the marriage bed kept pure, for God will judge the adultery and the sexually immoral." (Hebrews 13:4, NIV).

With the scriptural support of remarriage in an honorable manner, if the wife decides to remarry when the husband dies, it all up to her desires. If divorce happens because of the unfaithfulness of the other spouse in a marriage, it up to the desire of the spouse to remarry or can forgive each other and remarry the same husband or wife if they have reconciled. There is a particular clause in the Deuteronomy, "If a man marries a woman who becomes displeasing to him because he finds something indecent about her, and he writes her of a divorce, gives it to her and sends her from his house, and if after she leaves his house she becomes the wife of another man, and her second husband dislikes her and writes her a certificate of divorce, gives to her and sends her from his house, of if he dies, then her first husband, who divorced her, is not allowed to marry her again after she has been defiled. That would be detestable in the eyes of the Lord. Do not bring sin upon the land the Lord your God is giving you as an inheritance." (Deut. 24:1-4, NIV). Marriage is God's institution and it regarded as sacred by God and when marriage is threatened by divorce,

One of the fascination Scriptures in the Bible that is contextual and relevant to all Christians in every generation are the six instructions that Paul prescribe in (Philippians 4:4-9, NIV) are:

Rejoice: He should rejoice in the Lord always. Under all circumstances, which include suffering, frustration, depression, sadness, loss and abandonment, the counselee should rejoice in the Lord always. *Chairein* and *chaironton* are the same Greek word, *chairo* which means rejoice. It also means be glad, full of joy. Joy is God given and it is the fountain in the heart of the believer which is poured out by the Holy Spirit and it keeps on bubbling regardless of the situation or circumstances. It cannot be overwhelmed by the circumstances or situation around a belief. Paul talks about what can separate you from the Lord of God? He makes a conclusion, "Who shall separate us from the love of Christ? Shall trouble or hardship or persecution or famine or nakedness or danger or sword? ... Neither height nor depth, nor anything else in all creation will be able to separate us from the love of God that is in Christ Jesus our Lord," (Rom. 8:39, NIV).

Gentleness - To be gentle, is to be Christlike in character and conduct. The counselee must be gentle with others, loving, caring, tenderhearted, and to be considerate. The counselee should learn to put others first.

Anxious - Don't be anxious, self-centered. "Do not be anxious about anything, but in everything, by prayer and petition," (Phil. 4: 6, NIV). Being anxious means, you are worried, concerned, and uncertain what will happen next. The counselee should pray instead of being anxious and worried about the future. The counselee should put his trust in the Lord who cares for him, "Cast all your anxiety on him because he cares for you," (I Peter 5:7, NIV), (Psalm 34:4, NIV); "I want you to be free from anxieties," (I Cor. 7:32, ESV); "Say to those who have an anxious heart, 'Be strong; fear not! Behold, your God will come with vengeance, with the recompense of God. He will come and save you," (Isaiah 35:4, ESV).

Prayer - In prayer present your petition to God. We can communicate with God through prayer. Prayer simply is talking to God with your heart.

The counselee should be a prayerful man who is connected with God always. A good example of a prayerful person was our Lord Jesus Christ. He was always in touch with His Father. The counselee is taught to pray without ceasing, "Rejoice always, pray without ceasing, give thanks in all circumstances, for this is the will of God," (I Thess. 5:16-17, ESV).

Thanksgiving - Giving thanks to God is the reasonable service. The counselee is taught that thanksgiving is part of worship and he should give thanks to the Lord all the days of his life. There are always many reasons to give thanks to God as an attitude of gratitude for both spiritual and physical health. Some of the following Scriptures capture the essence of thanksgiving to God, "Enter his gates with thanksgiving and his courts with praise; give thanks to him and praise His Name," (Psalm 100:4, ESV); "Let us come before His presence with thanksgiving; Let us shout joyfully to Him with psalms," (Psalm 95:2-3, NKJV); "Oh, give thanks to the Lord, for he is good… For His mercy endures forever," (I Chronicles 16:34, NKJV), "Let them give thanks to the Lord for his wonderful deeds for wonderful deeds for mankind…" (Psalm 107:31, NIV).

Peace - The peace of God and tranquility will guard your heart and mind. The peace with God is essential for any counselee to be always in tune with God. When a sinner commits his life to Christ, he is given peace, the inner peace. The Hebrew word, *shalom*, means wholeness, welfare, prosperity, completeness, harmony and tranquility. Jesus said, "Peace I leave with you; my peace I give you. I do not give to you as the world gives," (John 14:27, ESV). Christ gives us eternal peace. The counselee is to be encouraged to seek the peace of God that will guard them.

Psychological Trauma of Regret Over Past Sin and God's Solution

I John 1:7-2:2, ESV, to the person living in regret over past sin.
I John 1:7-2:2, ESV, John encourages any person who is reliving his/her past sins with regrets by pointing to the redemption, grace and love that Christ offers to all sinners. John says either you are in the light or darkness. Those in the light love God and live and walk in the light. Those who are in the light live and in fellowship with God and one another and that the blood of

Christ purifies from all sin. That is the premise where John puts everything in the right perspective. In the following verses, 8-10, John challenges everyone who claims to be without sin, it is a self -deception and the truth is not within. Verse 9, points to the person living in regret over the past sin brought into the circle of Christ, "If we confess our sins, he is faithful and just and will forgive us our sins and purify us from all unrighteousness," (I John 1:10, ESV) This is good news to a person who lives in regret over the past sin because it tells the sinner what to do. First, if he/she confesses his/her sins, Christ is faithful and just to forgive our sins and purify us from all unrighteousness. John makes a distinction between sin in (v. 8) and sins in (v. 9). Sin refers to our sinful nature with corrupt and evil thoughts whilst sin refers to evils that we have done. Christ died for both our sins and our sin, the sin of omission and commission. He was covered all at once by His atonement for us (Heb. 10:4, ESV). The answer for someone living in regret over his/her past sin is that he/she has to confess with his/her mouth that he/she is a sinner, repent and believe in Christ Jesus. When he/she believes, has faith and puts his/her trust in Christ, God promises these: First, He is faithful, meaning He is trustworthy and dependable. Second, He is just, which means is impartial, fair yet sin must be punished. Third, He will forgive you all your sins which means, He will pardon all the past sins/wrongs you have committed in the past and He purifies us from all unrighteousness. This is good news for the counselee.

Verse 10, it's contrasting a person who is not willing to confess and repent from his/her sins, "If we claim we have not sinned, we make him a liar and his word has no place in our lives." This is a person who does not want to confess and repent from his/her sin. Those who do not want to acknowledge that they are sinners and confess and repent are not going to be pardoned. Chapter 2:1 categorically, we do not have to sin, however, if anyone sins, we have an advocate, one who speaks to the Father in our defense-Jesus Christ. He is the atoning sacrifice for our sins, and not only for ours but also for the sins of the whole world." The counselee has learned that his/her sins are forgiven, pardoned and has been justified by Christ for his/her past sins. His/her regrets over his/her past sins have been covered by Christ and He is also an advocate if ever he/she sins. He/she is now in the family of God in fellowship with God and other believers because of his/her confession, repentance and being adopted into the family of God.

CHAPTER SIX
GOD & NATION

God's Command to the Kings

People struggling with fear concerning world events, there is good news that God's sovereignty covers the entire globe and He watches the world events and He is in control of everything. He sent Son, Jesus Christ to redeem the people from their sins and to redeem the world because everything belongs to Him. First, "For God has not given us the spirit of fear, but of power; and of love, and soul mind," (II Timothy 1:7, NKJV). "There is no fear in love; but perfect love casts out fear, because fear hath torment. He who fears is not made perfect in love," (I John 4:18, NKJV). If a counselee is consumed with fear of the world events, it is important who he/she is in Christ. The counselee has to be reminded that God is in control of everything. "God changes times and seasons; he deposes kings, and raises up others. He gives wisdom to the wise and knowledge to the discerning," (Daniel 2:21, NIV).

I would assign him/her Scriptures to read and to come out with his/her findings in the following session and share what he/she would have discovered, such as (Daniel 2:21; I John 4:18; II Tim. 1:7, NIV). "The decision is announced by messengers, the holy ones declare the verdict, so that the living may know that the highest is sovereign over all kingdoms on earth and gives them to anyone he wishes and sets over them the lowliest of people," (Daniel 4:17, NIV). The love of God has been poured into us through the Holy Spirit. God's love is perfect, unconditional, faithful, forgiving, pure, everlasting, and encompassing. God's love is revealed in Christ Jesus. God's love is *agape* (Greek), the love which is sacrificial and unconditional. "Give thanks to the God of heaven, for his steadfast love endures forever," (Psalm 136:26, ESV). "Dear friends, let us love one another, for love comes from God. Everyone who loves has been born of God and knows God. Whoever does not love does not know God, because God is love," (I John 4:7-8, NIV). "For God so loved the world that He gave His only begotten Son, that whoever believes in Him should not perish but have everlasting life," (John 3:16, NKJV). God loved, and He demonstrated His love by giving His only Son. "We love Him because He first loved us," (I John 4:19, NKJV). It is important to talk about God's love during the counseling process so that the counselee understands and knows God's love available.

The justice of God is very clear that He is God of justice and He is impartial and kind but His judgment is righteous. "Righteous and justice are the foundation of your throne; steadfast love and faithfulness go before you," (Psalm 89:14, NIV). "For I, the Lord, love justice in the burnt offering..." (Isaiah 61:8, NKJV). "Surely God will never do wickedly, Nor will the Almighty pervert justice," (Job 34:12, NKJV). "He is the Rock, His work is perfect, for all His ways are just; A God of faithfulness and without injustice, Righteous and upright is He," (Deut. 32:4, NKJV). The Justice of God is one of God's attributes. It is important during counseling process to tell the counselee that God is a loving God but He is also God of justice, punishing the children for their parents, "For I, the Lord your God, am a jealous God, visiting the iniquity of the fathers upon the children to the third and fourth generations of those of those who hate Me," (Deut. 5:9, NKJV).

The providence of God is that He is Self-Sufficient, and He is Jehovah Jireh, the provider and sustainer of life. In the counseling process, the importance of God's providence needs to be shared with the counselee that He is omniscient all knowing, omnipotent all powerful, omnipresent always present not limited with space or location. The counselee needs to be encouraged that God is sufficient for every human problem and that He is always willing to engage with anyone who is willing to let Him in, (Rev. 3:20, NKJV). The sovereignty of God is His power, authority and justice over the universe and that He is omniscience, omnipotent and omnipresent. Therefore, the importance of God's sovereignty to the counseling process is that he is in control of every situation and destiny of the counselee and also the counselor. God's right and power rest on Him alone and whatever He decides will come to pass.

God's Command to Politicians

Politicians have put in their positions by God and they should work for the civil governments for the benefits of the citizens. The politicians should work for God and the people even though they in a secular world. The politicians should be aware to whom they give their allegiance to. God only deserves the honor, the praise, worship and the allegiance. "Blessed is the nation whose God is the Lord, the people He has chosen as His is own. inheritance. The Lord looks from heaven; He sees all the sons of men," (Psalm 33:12-13, NKJV). The politicians can be wicked and cruel towards the people they rule and God is not pleased with such conduct. "When the wicked rise to power, people go into hiding, the righteous thrive," (Proverbs 28:28, NIV). As the Creator of the universe, God is against the rulers who are not compassionate and kind to the populace of their nations. He wants justice to prevail. "When the righteous thrive, the people rejoice; when the wicked rule, the people groan," (Proverbs 29:2, NIV).

The politician should be aware not to fulfill Satan's agenda. Some governments do not give reverence to God. Satan is working in the world against God's agenda using the spiritual forces in the air because he is the prince of the air. Spiritual warfare is real and the Apostle Paul warns and makes us aware that we are not fighting against flesh and blood but against spirituality. "Put on the whole armor of God, that ye may be able to stand against the wiles of the devil. For we do not wrestle against flesh and blood, but against principles, against powers, against the rulers of the darkness of this age, against spiritual hosts of the wickedness in the heavenly places," (Eph. 6:11-12, KJV). The devil is working against the believers and we have to put the armor of God. "Resist the devil and he will flee from you. "Submit yourselves, therefore to God. Resist the devil, and he will flee from you," (James 4:7, ESV). Saturate your minds with the Holy Scriptures and learn not in your own understanding. "Trust in the Lord with all thine heart; and lean not unto thine own your understanding. In all thy ways acknowledge him, and he shall direct thy paths," Proverbs 3:5-6, KJV).

Satan is regarded as an angel who rebelled against God and puffed himself up and thought himself to be equal to God. Christian tradition refers to Isaiah 14:12, NKJV, and Ezekiel 28:12-15, NKJV, as referring to Satan. He is viewed as the angel who possessed great piety and beauty but fell with the hosts of angels. His name is the Devil, Satan, the old serpent in the Garden of Eden who influenced Eve and Adam to sin against God (Gen. 3:1-24, NKJV). Satan is the evil spirit who is the god of this world. "In whom the god of this world hath blinded the minds of the them which believe not, lest the light of the glorious gospel of Christ, who is the image of God, shine unto them," (II Cor. 4:4, KJV). Satan is the false god of this world. Apostle Paul refers to Satan with his demons as principalities, the powers, the rulers, spiritual hosts in heavenly places (Eph. 6:12-13, KJV).

"And no wonder, for Satan himself masquerades as an angel of light," (II Cor. 11:14, NIV). He comes as an angel of light but he is wicked and his schemes are deceptive and corrupt. "When he tells a lie, he speaks from his own nature, because he is a liar and the father of liars," (John 8:44, NKJV). Satan tempted Christ in the wilderness three times, on hedonism - hunger/satisfaction, egoism - specular/might, materialism - kingdoms/wealth (Matt. 4:1-11, NKJV). Be alert and of sober mind. Your enemy the devil prowls around like a roaring lion looking for someone to devour," (I Pet. 5:8, NKJV).

Death is the last enemy to be destroyed. "But it has now been revealed through the appearing of our Savior, Christ Jesus, who has destroyed death and brought life and immortality to light through the gospel, (II Tim. 1:10; Heb. 2.14; I Cor. 15:26, NIV). The devil will cast in the lack of fire. "And the devil, who has deceived them, was thrown into the lake of burning sulfur, where the beast and the false prophet had been thrown. They will be tormented day and night for and ever (Rev. 20:10, NIV). It is also important to note that, Christians are obligated to respect and to honor the government put by God. "Let everyone be subject to the governing authorities, for there is no authority except that which God has established by God. Consequently, whoever rebels against the authority is rebelling against what God has instituted, and those who do so will bring judgment on themselves," (Romans, 13:1-2, NIV). It is very clear that every government in authority has been put by God and all citizens should be submit to its rule. However, if the government violets justice and treat people unfairly, then it is no longer represent God and good governance.

God's Command to Social Justice

God is God of justice and God demands justice for every government to uphold justice and the sanctity of life. God has given mankind the governments to rule with justice and fairness because all human beings are God-image bearers hence, He wants everyone to be treated with dignity, mutual respect and honor. "But let justice run down like waters and righteousness like a mighty stream," (Amos 5:24, NKJV). God's justice is the standard everywhere and He requires fairness and rule of law instituted by the civil society. "Righteousness and justice are the foundation of your throne; Mercy and truth go before your face," (Psalm 89:14, NKKV). God's expectations from humankind are to do three things, "He has shown you, O mortal, what is good. And what does the Lord require of you? To act justly and to love mercy and to walk humbly with your God," (Micah 6:8, NIV). To understand God's mindset about His justice, we must understand and analyze His five attributes to show that He is watching every affair happening in the world because He is sovereign. The six attributes of God are categorized in two main sections, incommunicable attributes of God which are possessed by God alone, not any other which I will list. They are also communicable qualities of God that are possessed by both God and human beings, but not perfectly on the side of man. I will not list those that we resemble God. The six attributes of God:

1. **Infinite**- God's self-existence, without origin, self-sufficient, (Colossians 1:17; Psalm 147:5, NKJV).
2. **Immutable**- God never changes, He is always the same yesterday, today and forever. He changes not. He executes His plans as they are and He promises are always kept, (Romans 8:35-39, NKJV).
3. **Self-Sufficient**- God does not lack or need anything. He is not limited. He is complete and whole, and He has wisdom, power, authority, and goodness, (John 5:26; Gen. 17:1; Eph. 3:16, NKJV).

4. **Omnipotent**- God is all powerful and majesty. By His word, the heavens were created, (Psalm 33:6; Job 11:7-11; Heb. 6:18, NKJV). He has unlimited power.

5. **Omniscience**- God is all knowing because he remembers the past and the present at the same time. He says, "My purpose will stand and I will do all that I please," (Isaiah 46:9-10, NIV). "But the very hairs of your head are all numbered. Do not fear therefore; you are of more value than many sparrows, (Luke 12:7, NKJV).

6. **Omnipresent**- Everywhere is always in God's presence. "Where shall I go from your Spirit? Or where shall I flee from your presence," (Psalm 139:7, ESV). He is not limited by space or location. He is the Spirit. "Where can I go from your Spirit? Or where can I flee from your presence? If I ascend to heaven, you are there, If I make my bed in Sheol, behold, you are there. If I take the wings of the dawn, if I dwell in the remotest part of the sea, even there in your hand will lead me, and your right hand will lay hold of me." (Psalm 139:7-10; Jeremiah 23:23-24, NIV).

Nothing is hidden in His sight and He observes everyone and everywhere at the same time. He is not limited to time, space or location. Those who are on the thrones, governments, institutions, in leadership positions are the custodians of human affairs. They are representatives of God in many ways.

God's Command to Economists

For people to thrive and live happily to fulfill their purposes in lives, the economy of each country has to be producing enough products for the nation. The Gross Domestic Product which is the total market value of all final goods and services within a country. The monetary value of all the goods and services make the country to thrive. The sectors such as agriculture, mining, education, industry, health, commerce, technology, tourism, and human resources. The natural resources that God gave to each nation is for the benefit every citizen. The politicians who are in power they usually usurp and become greedy to get involved in corruption and taking the resources to themselves leaving the poor people poorer. As a result, the rich become more richer and the country may suffer economic slump. Corruption can wreck-havoc in the civil society if the laws of the land cannot protect the poor. Those who are rich need the same protection by the law of the land to do their businesses fairly and freely without any interference from the government as long as they follow the rules and the laws.

The government's main job is to create a conducive economic environment for gid and small businesses, entrepreneurship, industry, commerce to strive. When the population is involved in the economic development, it empowers the citizens to create wealth for themselves, for the society and to the nation at large. It all starts with families who are enabled to invest on their children through solid education as the foundation. Parents count the costs of their children. They start with analyzing cost effectiveness for their children. If their investment on children is not cost effective, that is, after completing their education, do the benefit from the education they offered to their children. If they don't benefit, it means their investment was not cost effective because if the cost exceeds the benefits, then it was not worth investing to the education of the children. However, if the benefits exceed the costs, then it means the investment to their children was cost effective. The cost benefit analysis should help the parents to invest to the scholarships of their children.

When the families prosper, the communities, societies and the nation prosper and is able to raise its Gross Domestic Product (GDP). God's family business includes the prosperity, health and wealth of the family that is enhanced by the family's spirituality. The sound economic stability of a country drives the families unity and prosperity. The family that prays, fellowship and assist each other, stick together. There goes the family, there goes the church and there goes the nation.

CONCLUSION

The book discusses God's idea of marriage and family which God designed for mankind and it found in the Bible, chapter one. In chapter two, discusses the blossom of the family when it starts, expectations of the husband, the wife and the children as the chart the way forward with their growth and vision. Chapter three highlights some of the fundamental and intricates of parenting children in diaspora with kinds of mixed cultures and new adaptations. Chapter four discusses choosing a life partner, specifically, for the youths and those who are mature and ready enter into marriage. It answers the five most important questions such why, who, where, and how to marry. Chapter five discusses marriage separation and divorce and chapter six, which is the last chapter, discusses God and the nation in which how God watches the events of the world and expects the governments instituted are obligated to govern with integrity, justice and mutual respect for every citizen. The book is packed with contemporary and relevant issues.

BIBLIOGRAPHY

Adams, Jay E. *Hope for the New Millenniums* (Woodruff, SC: Timeless Text, 1994), 15.

Adeyemo et al, Tokunboh, *African Bible Commentary* (Nairobi: World Alive Publishers, 2006 and Helwys, 2001), 385.

Bailey, Keith M. *Christ's Coming and His Kingdom* (Harrisburg, PA: Christian Publications, 1981

Calvin, John. *Commentary on Genesis, Commentaries on the First Book of Moses*, vol. 1 (Grand Rapids: Baker, 1996

Everstine, Louis. *The Anatomy of suicide: Silence of the Heart* (Springfield, WA: Charles C. Thomas, 1998

Gill, John, *An Exposition of First Book of Moses Called Genesis* (Lebanon, MO: Particular Baptist, 2010

Haldane, James A. *Hebrews*, Newport Commentary Series, 2nd ed. (Springfield, MO: Particular Baptist Press, 2002

Hamilton, James M. *Revelation: The Spirit Speaks to the Churches* (Wheaton, IL: Crossway, 2012

Hamilton, Victor P. *The Book of Genesis: Chapters 1-17*, The New International on the Old Testament (Grand Rapids: William B. Eerdmans, 1990

Hawthorne, Gerald F. and Martin, Ralph P. *Philippians*, Word Biblical Commentary, vol. 43 (Nashville: Nelson Reference and Electronic, 2004),

Henry, Carl, Baker's Dictionary of Christian Ethics, (USA: Canon Press, 1973),

Hodge, Charles. *2 Corinthians*, The Crossway Classic Commentaries (Wheaton, IL: Crossway, 2015

Hodges, Jesse Wilson. *Christ's Kingdom and Coming* (Grand Rapids: Wm. B. Eerdmans, 1957),

Ironside, Henry A. *I and 2 Corinthians, An Ironside Expository Commentary* (Grand Rapids: Kregel, 2006

Jacobs, Douglas and Brown, Herbert N. *Suicide: Understanding and Responding* (Madison, CT: International University Press, 1989

Johnson, Sheri L. and Hayes, Adele M. *Stress, Coping and Depression* (Mahwah, NJ: Lawrence Erlbaum Associates, 2000), ix.

Leupold, Herbert C. *Exposition of Genesis Chapters 1-19,* Christian Classics Ethereal (Grand Rapids: Baker, 1950

Lincoln, Andrew T. *Ephesians*, Word Biblical Commentary, vol. 42 (Dallas: Word, 1990

MacArthur, John. *Romans1-8, The MacArthur New Testament Commentary Series* (Chicago: Moody, 1983), 16.

Martin, Ralph P. *2 Corinthians*, Word Biblical Commentary, vol. 40, 2nd ed. (Grand Rapids: Zondervan, 2014

Mathews, Kenneth A. *Genesis 1-11:26*, The New American Commentary, vol. 1A (Nashville: Broadman & Holman, 1996

Mbiti, John S. African Religions and Philosophy, 2ⁿᵈ Edition, (Oxford: Heineman, 1969), 118.

McKeown, James. *Genesis,* Two Horizons Old Testament Commentary (Grand Rapids: William B. Eerdmans, 2008

Moule, Handley Carr. *Studies in Colossians and Philemon* (Grand Rapids: Kregel, 1977

Naylor, Peter. *A Study Commentary on 2 Corinthians* (Darlington, England: Evangelical, 2002)

O'Donovan, Wilbur. *Biblical Christianity in Modern Africa* (Carlisle: Paternoster Press, 2000

Papolos, Demitri F. and Papolos, Janice. *Overcoming Depression* (New York: Harper Perennial, 1992

Patterson, Paige. *Revelation*, The New American Commentary, vol. 39 (Nashville: B & H, 2012

Phillips, John. *Exploring Genesis, John Phillips Commentary Series* (Chicago: Moody, 1980

Price, James L. and Laymon, Charles M. eds., *Interpreter's One-Volume Commentary on the Bible* (Nashville: Abingdon, 1980.

Reddish, Mitchell G. *Revelation*, Smyth and Helwys Bible Commentary (Macon, GA: Smyth

Reno, Russell R. *Genesis,* Brazos Theological Commentary on the Bible (Grand Rapids: Brazos, 2010), 56

Rice, John R. *Genesis: "In the Beginning . . ."* (Murfreesboro, TN: Sword of the Lord, 1975

Sacks, Robert D. *A Commentary on the Book of Genesis,* Ancient Near Eastern Texts and Studies, vol. 6 (Lewiston, NY: Edwin Mellen, 1990

Sailhamer, John H. *Genesis,* in vol. 1 of *The Expositor's Bible Commentary,* ed. Gaebelein, Frank E. Kaiser, Walter C. and Hess. Richard. (Grand Rapids: Zondervan, 2008

Sailhamer, John H. *Genesis,* in vol. 2 of *The Expositor's Bible Commentary,* ed. Frank E. Gaebelein (Grand Rapids: Zondervan, 1990

Still, Todd D. *Philippians and Philemon,* Smyth and Helwys Bible Commentary (Macon, GA: Smyth and Helwys, 2011), 34.

Taylor, Mark. *1 Corinthians,* The New American Commentary, vol. 28 (Nashville: B & H, 2014

Taylor, Walter F. *Ephesians,* Augsburg Commentary on the New Testament (Minneapolis: Augsburg, 1985

Torre, Miguel De La *Genesis, Belief: A Theological Commentary on the Bible* (Louisville: Westminster John Knox, 2011

Uprichard, Harry. *A Study Commentary on Ephesians* (Darlington, England: Evangelical, 2004),

Von Rad, Gerhard. *Genesis: A Commentary,* trans. John H. Marks (Philadelphia: Westminster, 1961), 94.

Wall, Robert W. *Colossians and Philemon,* IVP New Testament, Commentary (Downer Groves, IL: IVP, 1993

Walton, John H. *Genesis,* The NIV Application Commentary (Grand Rapids: Zondervan, 2001

Wenham, Gordon J. *Genesis 1-15,* Word Biblical Commentary, vol. 1 (Waco, TX: Word, 1987

Wetzel, Janice Wood, *Clinical Handbook of Depression* (New York: Gardner,

Wilson, Daniel. *Expository on Colossians, Verse-by-Verse Bible Commentary* (New York: Bible House, 1859), 73.

Wright, Nicholas T. *Colossians and Philemon*, Tyndale New Testament Commentaries, vol. 1 (Downers Grove, IL: IVP, 1986

REFERENCES

American Psychiatric, www.psychiatry.org, and https://www.psychiatry.org/patients-families/ocd/what-is-obsessive-compulsive-disorderAccessed February 2, 2021).

American Psychiatric, www.psychiatry.org, and https://www.psychiatry.org/patients-families/ocd/what-is-obsessive-compulsive-disorderAccessed February 2, 2021.

American Psychological Association (Producer). (2009). Session 2 [Video segment]. In *Psychoanalytic Therapy Over Time* (DVD). *Series VIII – Psychotherapy in Six Sessions.* Retrieved January 10, 2019 from Walden Library, Database.

American Psychological Association (Producer). (2009). Session 2 [Video segment]. In *Psychoanalytic Therapy Over Time* (DVD). *Series VIII – Psychotherapy in Six Sessions.* Retrieved January 10, 2019 from Walden Library, Database.

American Psychological Association (Producer). (2012). *Interpersonal-relational integrative approach to working with men* [Video file]. Retrieved January 7, 2019 from Psychotherapy database.

American Psychological Association (Producer). (2012). *Interpersonal-relational integrative approach to working with men* [Video file]. Retrieved January 7, 2019 from Psychotherapy database.

Anchin, J. C., & Pincus, A. L. (2010). Evidence-based interpersonal psychotherapy with personality disorders: Theory, components, and strategies. In J. J. Magnavita (Ed.), *Evidence-based treatment of personality dysfunction: Principles, methods, and processes* (pp.

113–166). Washington, DC: American Psychological Association. doi:10.1037/12130-00, Retrieved January 10, 2019 from the Walden Library databases.

Anchin, J. C., & Pincus, A. L. (2010). Evidence-based interpersonal psychotherapy with personality disorders: Theory, components, and strategies. In J. J. Magnavita (Ed.), *Evidence-based treatment of personality dysfunction: Principles, methods, and processes* (pp. 113–166). Washington, DC: American Psychological Association. doi:10.1037/12130-00, Accessed January 10, 2019 from the Walden Library databases.

Caligor, E., Kernberg, O.F., & Clarkin, J. F. (2007). *Handbook of dynamic psychotherapy for higher level personality pathology.* Washington, D.C.: American Psychiatric Publishing. Retrieved January 9, 2021 from Walden Database.

Caligor, E., Kernberg, O.F., & Clarkin, J. F. (2007). *Handbook of dynamic psychotherapy for higher level personality pathology.* Washington, D.C.: American Psychiatric Publishing. Accessed January 9, 2019 from Walden Database.

https://docs.google.com/document/d/1ORRkug4KmbcJq6wsiMkuZoe2w JGLNy4ESvnVjjfXsJc/edit, Accessed February 2, 2021.

Mateo and Luna Sol, (2012-2018), https://lonerwolf.com/contact, (Accessed February 26, 2021).

McCann and Landers, (2010), https://www.ncbi.nlm.nih.gov/pmc/articles/ PMC2856099/#R48.

Medical News Today, https://www.medicalnewstoday.com, Accessed February 2, 2021.

New Jersey Gallup's Annual Polls on Values and beliefs in America, https:// news.gallup.com/poll/23404/ideal-age-marriage-women-men. aspx), Accessed, March 1, 2021.

R. Ingall and N. Oliver, "Depression—A Misunderstood Illness: Understanding and Treating Depression," accessed January 9, 2021, www.Depression- a Misunderstood Illness: Understanding and Treating Depression.

R. Ingalla and N. Oliver, "Depression Beater/ Understanding Depression," 12, accessed January 8, 2021, http://www.depressionbeater.com/ Understanding-Depression,(2270954

Safran, J. D. (1993). Breaches in the therapeutic alliance: An arena for negotiating authentic relatedness. *Psychotherapy, 30*(1), 11–24. Accessed January 3, 2021.

Safran, J. D. (1993). Breaches in the therapeutic alliance: An arena for negotiating authentic relatedness. *Psychotherapy, 30*(1), 11–24. Accessed January 3, 2021.

Safran, J. D., & Muran, J. C. (2000). *Negotiating the therapeutic alliance: A relational treatment guide.* New York, NY: Guilford Press. Accessed January 9, 2021, from Walden Library Database.

Safran, J. D., & Muran, J. C. (2000). *Negotiating the therapeutic alliance: A relational treatment guide.* New York, NY: Guilford Press. Accessed January 9, 2021, from Walden Library Database.

Stuart Scott and Heath Lambert, *Counseling the Hard Cases*, (Nashville: B & H Publishers), 2012, p. 266

Teyber, E., & Teyber, F. H. (2017). *Interpersonal process in therapy: An integrative model* (7th ed.). Belmont, CA: Brooks/Cole. Retrieved January 2, 2019 from Walden Library database.

Teyber, E., & Teyber, F. H. (2017). *Interpersonal process in therapy: An integrative model* (7th ed.). Belmont, CA: Brooks/Cole. Retrieved January 2, 2019 from Walden Library database.